Getting old in Ancient Egypt

Cover illustration: The family of the workman Pashedu preceded by his white haired father and greying mother. From the Theban tomb of Pashedu (TT 3), Nineteenth Dynasty (Photograph courtesy of Dr. Alain-Pierre Zivie).

Dedicated to
Dr. I.E.S. Edwards
The Nestor of British Egyptology
in affection and esteem

Getting old
in Ancient Egypt

Rosalind M. and Jac. J. Janssen

 The Rubicon Press

The Rubicon Press
57 Cornwall Gardens
London SW7 4BE

British Library Cataloguing in Publication Data

ISBN 0-948695-46-3 (hbk)
ISBN 0-948695-47-1 (pbk)

Designed by Screentype, London
Printed and bound in Great Britain by Biddles Limited of Guildford
and King's Lynn

Contents

List of Illustrations

Theban tomb of Pashedu (TT 3), Nineteenth Dynasty (Courtesy of Dr. Alain-Pierre Zivie).

11. Limestone statuette of an undernourished potter squatting at his wheel. From the mastaba of Nikauinpu at Giza, Fifth to Sixth Dynasty (OI 10628. Courtesy of the Oriental Institute of the University of Chicago).

12. Skeleton of Idu II lying in his cedar coffin. From the mastaba of Idu II at Giza, Sixth Dynasty (PM 2639/2511. Courtesy of the Roemer-Pelizaeus Museum, Hildesheim).

13. Skeletons of elderly women, each accompanied by a pot. From a Predynastic Cemetery at Naga ed-Deir (a) Tomb N 7140; (b) Tomb N 7081 (after Lythgoe, *The Predynastic Cemetery N 7000: Naga-ed-Dêr*, IV, 1965, figures 17f and 33i).

14. The third entry of the houselist when Snefru was head of the family. From Kahun, Thirteenth Dynasty (UC 32163. Courtesy of the Petrie Museum of Egyptian Archaeology, University College London).

15. Two clusters of houses in the Southern zone of el-Amarna. Nos. N 49.9 and N 50.29 (after Borchardt and Ricke, *Die Wohnhäuser in Tell el-Amarna*, 1980, plan 73).

16. Group of elderly men sitting in the shade. West Bank of Luxor, 1996 (Photograph by Rosalind Janssen).

17. The lower half of the Second Kamose stela depicting the overseer of the seal Neshi, the ancestor of Mose. From Karnak, late Seventeenth Dynasty (Photograph courtesy of the late Dr. Labib Habachi; now Luxor Museum J.43).

18. Limestone *akh iqer en Re* stela of Dhutymose. From Deir el-Medina, Twentieth Dynasty (UC 14228. Courtesy of the Petrie Museum of Egyptian Archaeology, University College London).

19. Wooden anthropoid busts: (a) with short hair. From tomb 136 at Sedment, Eighteenth Dynasty (UC 16554. Courtesy of the Petrie Museum of Egyptian Archaeology, University College London); (b) with tripartite wig. Unprovenanced, New Kingdom (UC 16550. Courtesy of the Petrie Museum of Egyptian Archaeology, University College London).

20. Funerary procession: four men carry a canopic shrine on a sledge (right), two men with anthropoid busts (centre), followed by a man with a mummy mask and a necklace (left). From the Theban tomb of Haremhab (TT 78), Eighteenth Dynasty (after Brack and Brack, *Das Grab des Haremheb. Theben Nr.78*, 1980, plate 61c).

21. Pottery dish inscribed on the interior with a Letter to the Dead. From tomb Y84 at Hu, First Intermediate Period (UC 16244. Courtesy of the Petrie Museum of Egyptian Archaeology, University College London).

22. Painted wooden statuette of Ankhiry against the Letter to the Dead. From Saqqara, Nineteenth Dynasty (AH 115 and AMS 64. Courtesy of

From the tomb of Ay at el-Amarna, Eighteenth Dynasty (after Davies, *The Rock Tombs of El Amarna*, VI, 1908, plate XXX).

37. Relief of Hesysunebef with a pet monkey, on the side of a fragmentary seated statue of Neferhotep and his wife Ubekht. From the Theban tomb of Neferhotep (TT 216), Nineteenth Dynasty (after Bruyère, *Rapport sur les fouilles de Deir el Médineh (1923-1924)*, 1925, figure 1 on p.41).

38. Mery-aa and his wives: (above) Mery-aa himself with his ?first wife Isi; (below) his five other wives. From the tomb of Mery-aa at el-Hagarseh, Ninth Dynasty (after Petrie, *Athribis*, 1908, plate VII).

39. Djau stands face to face with his father Djau/Shemay, who holds a *medu*-staff. From the tomb of Djau at Deir el-Gebrawi, Sixth Dynasty (after Davies, *The Rock Tombs of Deir El Gebrâwi*, II, 1902, plate X).

40. Limestone ostracon relating the charity shown by a man to a divorced woman. From Deir el-Medina, Twentieth Dynasty (UC 19614. Courtesy of the Petrie Museum of Egyptian Archaeology, University College London).

41. Limestone statue of Maya wearing the 'gold of honour'. From ?Akhmim, Eighteenth Dynasty (Inv.-Nr.19286. Courtesy of the Ägyptisches Museum und Papyrussammlung [Bode-Museum], Berlin).

42. Anhermose dressed as High Priest. From the tomb of Anhermose at el-Mashayikh, Nineteenth Dynasty (after Ockinga and al-Masri, *Two Ramesside Tombs at El Mashayikh*, I, 1988, plate 53).

43. Nebamun (left) receives his appointment to police chief from the royal scribe Iuny. From the Theban tomb of Nebamun (TT 90), Eighteenth Dynasty (after Davies, *The Tombs of Two Officials of Tuthmosis the Fourth (Nos. 75 and 90)*, 1923, plate XXVI).

44. King Neuserre carried in the Upper Egyptian palanquin. From the Sun-Temple of Neuserre at Abu Ghurab, Fifth Dynasty (after Von Bissing and Kees, *Das Re-Heiligtum des Königs Ne-Woser-Re*, II, *Die kleine Festdarstellung*, 1923, plate II).

45. Limestone lintel depicting the Sed Festival of Sesostris III. From the Temple of Montu at Medamud, Twelfth Dynasty. (after Lange and Hirmer, *Egypt*, 1956, plates 102-103; now Egyptian Museum, Cairo JE 56497).

46. Limestone block depicting Amenhotep III running the ceremonial course before Amen-Re. From the Open Air Museum at Karnak, Eighteenth Dynasty (Photograph by Rosalind Janssen).

47. Calcite (Egyptian alabaster) statuette of Pepy I. From Saqqara, Sixth Dynasty (39.120. Courtesy of the Brooklyn Museum, New York).

48. Limestone statue of Montuhotep II Nebhetepre in his *Heb-sed* garb. From the causeway of the Montuhotep Temple at Deir el-Bahri, Eleventh Dynasty (Photograph by Rosalind Janssen).

49. Limestone unfinished triad recently identified as Amenhotep III, Tiye,

and Beketaten. From el-Amarna, Eighteenth Dynasty (UC 004. Courtesy of the Petrie Museum of Egyptian Archaeology, University College London).

Amun, give me your heart
Direct towards me your ears
Open your eye
Save me every day
and lengthen for me my lifetime.

A prayer by a certain Penpare, written on the rock near the entrance to the Royal Cache (the so-called Tomb) of Inhapi at Western Thebes.

Acknowledgements

We are most grateful to the many museum curators who have provided us with photographs, in many cases gratis, and permission for their publication. Each institution is fully credited in the List of Illustrations. However, we would especially like to single out Dr. Bettina Schmitz of the Roemer-Pelizaeus Museum, Hildesheim, Dr. Stephen Quirke of the British Museum, London, and Mr. Robert Partridge whose help with photographs has been exceptional. Our special thanks must go to Dr. Alain-Pierre Zivie, who most kindly and at great speed sent us two of his superb colour transparencies. One has become our cover illustration, while the other appears as a black and white figure within the text. Ms Mary Hinkley of the Photography and Illustration Centre, University College London, painstakingly and with good humour, produced our other photographs. Ms Bram Calcoen is to be thanked and congratulated for her skilful line drawings and ever constant attention to detail.

To Anthea Page, Juanita Homan, and Robin Page, Partners of The Rubicon Press, we express our sincere gratitude. Once again, they have given us their habitual encouragement and assistance at every stage of the production.

Finally, we would like to thank all those who expressed an interest in our *Growing up in Ancient Egypt* which encouraged us to write the present volume.

Preface

This book is a sequel to our *Growing up in Ancient Egypt*, (London, 1990), and deals with the other extremity of human life. Like its counterpart, it is intended for the general reader, not for the professional Egyptologist. Therefore, despite some critical remarks made in personal conversation and in reviews of our former publication (primarily Gay Robins in the *Journal of Egyptian Archaeology* 80 [1994]), we have again decided not to encumber the present volume with a plethora of notes referring to the scientific works we consulted. Our colleagues should not need them; they are capable of recognizing our sources themselves, while lay people would hardly enjoy them, even if they could ever track down these studies. The bibliography at the end may be of some help, but the reader should bear in mind that it is merely a small selection from the numerous works we have consulted.

As before, our translations are mostly based on those of the admirable volumes by Miriam Lichtheim, *Ancient Egyptian Literature* (Berkeley, 1973-1980); in the last chapter also on her *Ancient Egyptian Autobiographies* (Freiburg/Göttingen, 1988).

Even more than was the case with childhood, old age has been a neglected subject in Egyptology. One reason for that is clear: the Egyptians never stressed that the elderly as such were a source of wisdom, as is the case in other ancient civilizations, such as those of India and China. On the one hand, lack of precursors made our task more difficult; we had ourselves to decide what subjects we wanted to discuss. There are indeed articles dealing with the topics of various chapters – they are quoted in the bibliography – but only a few. That meant, on the other hand, that we felt justified in using the opportunity to investigate all manner of aspects of Egyptian life which are in some way or other connected with old age. The present book is thus to a certain extent an introduction to Egyptology in general. This may be warranted since the elderly were, far more than children, part of the rich panorama of life in those days.

In our choice of illustration we have once again attempted to avoid the obvious, although it was not always easy to evade the well-known pictures. At the very least, all our photographs and line drawings illustrate parts of the text.

As was the case with our former common enterprise, composing this book was a particular pleasure to the authors. If, as we hope will be the case, the reader also enjoys the volume, then we have succeeded in our aim. That writing together as a married couple sometimes causes minor frictions in daily life will be readily understood, but our paramount feeling now that the book is completed is one of happiness and mutual affection.

February 1996   Rosalind and Jac. Janssen

Note to the translations:
Round brackets ( ) indicate: our explanations.
Square brackets [ ] indicate: restorations in the text.

Introduction
Gerontology

This is a book about getting old. The question immediately arises: who is old? A simple definition is one which we recently happened to hear on Radio 4's 'Thought for the Day'. "One is old if when bending down to tie up one's shoelaces, one looks around to see what else can be done on the floor before stretching up again". This picture reveals the physical, and also to some extent the psychological aspect of being elderly, as well as being an individual point of view. Of course, there are other, better definitions.

When asked who in our society are the aged, people are apt to come up with specific ages: those over sixty, or sixty-five, the moment in life when most of us have to retire. Two centuries ago our forebears would have answered very differently, for when old age pensions were first proposed in Britain, by Defoe in the 1690s, and by Dowdeswell in 1772, fifty was the age at which they were to be payable. These are administrative boundary lines.

But what is the criterion in societies where people do not know their exact age, as was the case in Ancient Egypt? Then functional definitions are used, based on performance rather than on age. For instance, individuals who cannot be fully productive any more are considered to be old; those not able to execute the full range of tasks appropriate to adults of one's sex and status, and, consequently, having to rely on others for part of their livelihood. The first stage of old age, those with much still to offer, is now sometimes called "young old". The next one, that of total dependence, requiring custodial care and supervision, either for physical or mental reasons, is known as "old old". A recently coined, but rather vague expression is that of "The Third Age". One of us recently gave a guided tour to the University of the Third Age, and was told by its lively participants: "We are really just a bunch of old fogeys"!

Other indications that one has passed the boundary line are, for instance, for a woman the end of the menopause, and for both men and women the birth of the first grandchild. Further physical indications occur, for example, the appearance of wrinkles and grey hair, or the onset of various ailments, usually in combination with each other. These include arthritis and rheumatism, breathlessness and giddiness, deafness, poor eyesight, forgetfulness, or even senility.

The academic discipline that is devoted to the study of ageing is called gerontology. It is a relative newcomer to the scholastic fraternity, yet it has already in its short history, produced a wealth of literature. The bibliography of a recent introductory work of less than 300 pages lists over 750 titles! A few of these pertinent publications are cited in our bibliography.

The enormous growth in gerontology should not surprise us: the rapidly expanding mass of elderly people in our modern world is one of its most spectacular features. Whereas at the beginning of the century the life expectancy for men was 44.1 years, and for women 47.8 years, this has risen to 72.4 and 78.1 years respectively. Looking at non-western, non-industrial societies, the contrast with the modern world is impressive: there those over sixty-five constitute one or two per cent of the population, in Britain that figure is at present over twenty per cent, and it will rise to about twenty-five per cent early in the next century. It is obvious that this situation creates numerous problems, and, consequently, leads to all kinds of researches.

Getting old exhibits various aspects: biological (what happens to our bodies in the course of our lives, and why); psychological (how do people react to their old age, and how do the circles in which they move react to them); social (which social and cultural factors influence the ageing process; what is the place of older people in a particular society). Several key subjects elicit much attention. Firstly, the medical problems, which are the object of a special branch of medicine called geriatrics. Then, for instance, the difficulties connected with retirement, such as a lower income and the loss of regular employment; or the need for adapted housing, and special homes for those who become totally dependent. Quite a different branch of study is the image of the aged in society: formerly preponderantly the aversion against senility and decrepitude, but recently also the attraction of leisure, enjoying a good pension and having the time and resources to travel all over the world. An aspect not (yet?) found in Britain, but present in some countries on the continent, is the foundation of political parties engaged entirely with the interests of senior citizens.

Gerontology deals with our society, and particularly with such practical problems. The study of ageing in other societies belongs to other disciplines, mainly social anthropology and history. There old people have a rarity value, since only a minority in the population reaches the age of seventy or even sixty. Those who do obviously possess exceptional qualities, perhaps even supernatural ones, and they are respected for them. Moreover, the long experience of the aged makes them repositories of vital information, both of a practical and of a ritual nature. They may even acquire a monopoly of strategic knowledge since they remember how one should act in the event of catastrophes.

Gerontology teaches us that there are two theories concerning the process of successful ageing: the activity theory, namely to maintain reasonable activity levels and substitute new rôles for those lost with retirement; and the disengagement theory that states that, as a person ages, a mutual withdrawal takes place between that individual and the society of which he is a part. Both attitudes are encountered in other civilizations. In Imperial China, for instance, old age was venerated and afforded a position of power, perhaps more than anywhere else. In India, however, we find the ideal of withdrawal, although mainly for the élite, and for men. The aged are supposed to retreat to the forest, renouncing all worldly attachments and becoming ascetics who retire into meditation.

As will appear evident in the following pages, our sources exhibit nothing of the latter attitude in Pharaonic Egypt. Neither is there any trace of a gerontocracy such as that which dominates some African societies. Nor is the wisdom of the elderly stressed, not even in the so-called Wisdom Literature. Being pre-eminently a literary civilization, even though the number of those able to read and write was limited to one or two per cent, the emphasis was placed firmly on the wisdom of the ancestors, particularly the great administrators of olden days.

In the *Instruction for Merikare* (see p. 92), we read:

> Copy your fathers, your ancestors,
> [for work is carried out through] knowledge.
> See, their words endure in books.
> Open and read them, copy their knowledge.
> He who is taught becomes skilled.

This means that in Ancient Egypt the rôle of the elderly was decidedly less conspicuous than in most other great civilizations. No doubt this goes a long way to explaining why no books have been devoted to the subject. Nevertheless, it is of fundamental importance to study this aspect of life in Pharaonic society, and the following pages are an attempt to redress the situation.

I Perceptions of the Older Generation

Some Egyptian texts contain a clear description of what it means to become old. The most famous of them is probably that at the beginning of the *Instruction of Ptahhotep* (see pp. 73-74 and 83). Ptahhotep, who was a Fifth Dynasty vizier under Pharaoh Isesi, speaks to his sovereign as follows:

> O King, my Lord!
> Old age is here, high age has arrived,
> Feebleness came, weakness grows,
> Childlike one sleeps all day.
> Eyes are dim, ears are deaf,
> Strength is waning, one is weary,
> The mouth, silenced, speaks not,
> The heart, void, recalls not the past,
> The bones ache throughout.
> Good has become evil, all taste is gone,
> What age does to people is bad in every respect.
> The nose, clogged, cannot breathe,
> Painful are standing and sitting.

This is indeed a moving picture of incipient decrepitude! Yet, it is not unique in the pages of world literature. Ageing is poignantly described in the *Panchatantra*, a famous collection of framing stories, animal fables and rhymed maxims, intended to teach practical politics and worldly wisdom. Created in India in the early centuries A.D., the work is known in several versions and in numerous translations. We quote here from the version of Arthur Ryder:

> Slow, tottering steps the strength exhaust,
>   The eye unsteady blinks,
> From drivelling mouth the teeth are lost,
>   The handsome figure shrinks,
> The limbs are wrinkled; relatives

and wife contemptuous pass;
The son no further honour gives
to doddering age. Alas!

Obviously, the impression made by the "old old" is the same in every civilization.

Ptahhotep's lamentation found an echo in the famous *Story of Sinuhe*, the literary autobiography of a fictitious courtier of the time of Amenemhat I and Sesostris I, known from many copies on papyri and ostraca. Its hero, after his flight to Syro-Palestine, dreams about his return:

Would that my body was young again!
For old age has come, feebleness has overtaken me.
My eyes are heavy, my arms weak;
My legs fail to follow.
The heart is weary; death is near.

The words seem to be inspired by the example of Ptahhotep. Or should we rather say that the picture of old age was so evident in those days that every author could have found his inspiration in the reality around him?

Yet, this was not the only possible manner in which to portray the aged. There is, for instance, an old magician called Djedi who occurs in the *Tales of Wonder*, featuring in the Papyrus Westcar, a Middle Kingdom collection of stories, now in Berlin (see p. 67). He is greeted by Prince Hardedef with flattering words, such as are eminently suitable for a venerable elderly person:

Your condition is like that of one who lives above age – for old age is the time of death, enwrapping, and burial – one who sleeps till daytime, free of illness, without a hacking cough.

Not everyone is therefore seen as a victim of his advanced years, although Djedi was certainly an exception. Was what the Egyptians saw daily around them so frightening that they needed to offset it by such an exaggerated story?

Descending from the lofty realms of poetry to the everyday vernacular, we should now look at the words in the Egyptian language by which the concept "old" was expressed. The most common one is written as *iau*, but, as is habitually the case, its actual pronunciation is quite uncertain. In most texts it is determined by the hieroglyphic sign of an elderly person – mostly a man, but occasionally a woman – bending over and leaning on a stick. We will discuss it further below (see p. 70 and fig. 28a and c).

A second word, *teni*, seems to carry the same meaning. Linguists, however, teach us that no two words in a language ever express exactly the same nuance. They usually have a different distribution, that is, they are not used in the same type of context. Hence, there will be some distinction between *iau* and *teni*, such as between our "old" and "elderly". But what exactly this could be unfortunately eludes us.

A third word for roughly the same concept, *kèhkèh*, indicates the physical aspect of getting old. Its original meaning may be "hacking cough", reproducing the throaty sound made by old people. As "hacking cough" it appears as the last word of the greeting to Djedi in the Papyrus Westcar, translated above. That it, in a wider sense, points to the bodily state of the elderly can be illustrated by a sentence in a magical papyrus from the New Kingdom, housed in the British Museum. Here the speaker derides his adversary with the words: "Your appearance is that of a monkey after reaching old age" (*kèhkèh*).

Another instance occurs in a literary work from el-Hiba, in Middle Egypt, which is dated to the Twenty-First Dynasty, and is now housed in the Pushkin Museum in Moscow (see p. 68). It is a tale concerning the wanderings of an outcast, presented in the form of a letter to a friend of his. In the initial lines the sender, according to the custom, wishes the addressee to reach the 110 years that constituted the ideal age (see p. 68), while "Your body is whole, grown old (*kèhkèh*) with a contented heart, without illness in your frame but continuous gladness and joy in your heart, and without the weakness of old age, you having arrested it". Once again the threat of the deterioration of the body is perceptible behind the words.

It is conspicuous that here both the words for old, namely *iau* and *kèhkèh*, are written with a sign that determines expressions of disease, pain, and such like. Its use, even more than the words themselves, reveal the feelings of the Ancient Egyptians towards old age.

The same sign, perhaps depicting a pustule or a gland, is also used, in combination with the hieroglyph of a man leaning on his stick, in the writing of *iau* in the so-called *Onomasticon of Amenope*. This is a glossary of hundreds of words, arranged in more or less consistent classes, describing all sorts of entities in the world. Several manuscripts of this list have survived, the most complete being known as the Golenisheff Onomasticon. Dating from the very end of the New Kingdom, it is also housed in the Pushkin Museum in Moscow. One of the classes are words for the different stages of the life of human beings. Starting with "man",

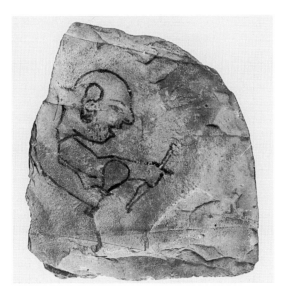

Limestone ostracon depicting an out of breath elderly workman cutting into the rock (Deir el-Medina, Ramesside Period). (Fig. 1)

there follow: "young man" (*iau*), "woman" and "young woman". The next group comprises various words for children, boys and girls. No special word for "old woman" is listed; one simply used the feminine form of *iau*. The division of life into three stages: young, adult, and old, reminds us of the modern expression "The Third Age" for the elderly. But for the Egyptians adolescence was a separate stage, distinguished from childhood as well as adulthood.

The deterioration of one's body was feared, as we saw above, but that was no reason to accept the treatment of the elderly as inferior beings. In a little known wisdom text we read: "You should not mock an old man or woman when they are decrepit (*kèhkèh*). Beware lest they [take action] against you before you get old". This warning is found on an ostracon now in the Petrie Museum of Egyptian Archaeology at University College London.

"Ostracon" (plural: ostraca) is the Greek word for potsherd. In Egyptology it is used for sherds which are inscribed with a hieratic (cursive form of hieroglyphs) text, but also for flakes of limestone bearing a drawing or an inscription in ink. Those that have survived from the Pharaonic Period – and there are several thousands of them – almost all derive from the settlement of the necropolis workmen at Western Thebes. These artisans built and decorated the tombs of the New Kingdom Pharaohs in the Valley of the Kings, as well as the burial places of members of the royal family in the Valley of the Queens. The draughtsmen among them were talented artists, as evidenced by numerous pictorial ostraca (fig. 1). These people lived in a village halfway between those two valleys, which is known by its Arabic name of Deir el-Medina. It is, as will become evident in this book, our main source of knowledge concerning daily life in Ancient Egypt, and it is the ostraca in particular which provide us with details unknown from elsewhere, for instance about old age.

Related to the documents from this village, but yet of a different type, are the so-called Tomb Robbery papyri (see p. 89). One of them, now in the British Museum, relates a story from which it appears that the respect for the elderly, mentioned in the Petrie ostracon, was by no means a universal practice.

A certain incense-roaster, named Shedsukhons, is interrogated by the vizier. He relates how he was visited by night in his house by some men. They urged him to go with them, and so they went to a tomb, opened it, robbed the gold and silver it contained, and divided the loot among them. Then, not unexpectedly, a quarrel arose concerning the division of the spoils. Shedsukhons' father started meddling in the matter, whereupon one of the thieves retorted: "O doddering old man, evil be his old age; if you are killed and thrown into the water, who will look for you?". Not exactly a friendly repartee, but what could the old man expect from such rough scoundrels?

Both attitudes we have observed, that of respect for elderly men and that of derision for the decaying body, are also encountered in the representations. An example of the former is found in the tomb of Sennefer (TT 96), the Theban mayor in the time of Amenhotep II. While in all other wall scenes he appears as a vigorous adult, one portrays him with rolls of fat along his torso (fig. 2). The implication is that he was a venerable elderly man. The opposing facet occurs in the tomb of Paheri, a mayor of el-Kab and Esna under Tuthmosis I. On a wall showing a series of agricultural scenes, we come across a pot-bellied old man with a receding hairline, who is combing flax (fig. 3). Convinced of the value of his performance, he says to a younger colleague who brings a bundle: "If you bring me thousands of bundles, I will still comb them". The other, clearly not impressed, answers: "Hurry up, don't chatter so much, you old baldy yokel".

As we stated in the Introduction, wisdom is not particularly stressed as a characteristic of the elderly. Yet, it is not wholly absent from the texts. On a Middle Kingdom stela from Edfu, which bears the autobiography of a priest called Tjeni, we read: "I am a trustworthy man for my brothers and sisters, old of heart, but one who does not know the weakness that belongs to it". That is, Tjeni states that he is wise, but not yet senile.

The elderly Sennefer holding a stick (Tomb of Sennefer (TT 96), Eighteenth Dynasty). (Fig. 2)

Such statements are rare. There is, however, one figure who was very probably elderly and who was believed to possess a deep knowledge of the secrets of life, far above that of most people who are apt to be confused by them. So far as we know, this figure was always a woman. There are not many places where a Wise Woman is mentioned, and those we know of all happen to derive from Deir el-Medina. There she was asked to bring enlightenment into situations in which people felt threatened and uncertain.

By their very nature such matters tend to be mysterious, and the documents which relate them are far from clear. They do not reveal the background of the various incidents and contain allusions which we do not understand. Therefore we can catch no more than glimpses of this particular rôle of elderly women in society.

One ostracon, now in a private collection in France, bears a letter written by a certain Qenkhopshef, one of the necropolis workmen, to a woman called Inerwau, who is otherwise unknown. It runs as follows:

Why did you not go to the Wise Woman
on account of the two boys who died in your charge?
Ask the Wise Woman about the death
the two boys have incurred.
'Was it their fate? Was it their destiny?'
You shall question (her) for me about them.
You shall (also) look after the life of mine
and the life of their mother.
As regards whatever god of which one will [speak] to you,
you shall afterwards write me his name.
[You shall fulfil] the task of one who knows her duty.

Qenkhopshef, evidently the father of the two boys who have died, wonders why Inerwau, perhaps their nurse, did not on her own initiative consult the Wise Woman. He wants to know why they died, and whether his life and that of their mother is now in danger. He especially wishes to hear which deity was responsible for his misfortune, hoping that the Wise Woman can at least give him some assurance in his misery.

Another ostracon, formerly in the collection of the distinguished Egyptologist Sir Alan Gardiner and now in the Ashmolean Museum in Oxford, is more obscure. A woman, whose name is not mentioned, states:

I went to the Wise Woman,
and she said to me:
'The manifestation of Ptah is with you,
because of the Light,
on account of an oath by his wife ....'

An old man combing flax (Tomb of Paheri at el-Kab, Eighteenth Dynasty). (Fig. 3)

11

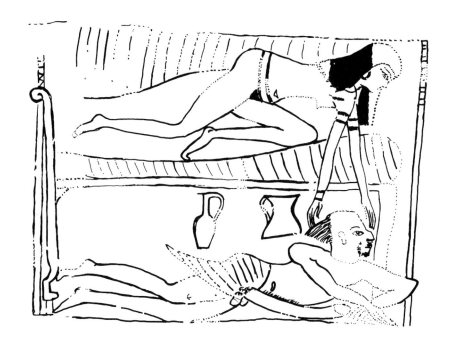

The Satirical-Erotic Papyrus; a girl attempts to seduce an exhausted man lying under her bed (Deir el-Medina, New Kingdom). (Fig. 4)

In this case the lady who turned to a Wise Woman was visited by what was called "the manifestation of Ptah". What exactly this means we do not know, but such manifestations of deities are also mentioned in other texts. In some instances we gain the impression that they haunted the dreams of those inflicted, but whether that was also the case here remains obscure. Who is meant by "the Light" which seems to be the cause of the lady's distress we likewise do not know. It may be a Pharaoh who is sometimes called so, either the ruling sovereign or the patron of the community, King Amenhotep I, or perhaps the sun-god Re who can also be addressed by this term.

A man seems also to be involved, for we hear of an oath by his wife. Is the lady who wrote the text accused of adultery? One can easily create a whole scenario out of the somewhat scanty evidence, but all we can really understand is that a Wise Woman was consulted in such a situation. She was thought to be able to provide the answers to all kinds of burning questions.

Venerated by some as possessors of esoteric knowledge, or simply considered to be wise, the elderly were therefore not to be scorned for the deterioration of their bodies. However, as we have seen, they were clearly regarded with disdain by others; despised, or even ridiculed. From Deir el-Medina comes a papyrus, now in Turin, which bears two series of drawings. On the right-hand side are representations of animals in human attitudes, whereas the continuation left bears twelve scenes of an outrageously erotic character. They tell the story of a man, shown with an oversized phallus, visiting a brothel and having intercourse in various positions with a prostitute.

The papyrus as it is now, exhibits numerous lacunae, also in the hieratic captions to the scenes, so that the whole is difficult to reconstruct. Fortunately, during the last century, when it was more complete, copies were made and these enable us to recognize what has been drawn. Because of its erotic nature, illustrations of this document have remained tabu, even in the scientific literature, until fairly recently.

There has been much discussion about various aspects of this unique papyrus. It has been suggested that it is mainly satirical, as, for instance, the position of the girl on a chariot would imply, since normally only the king rides alone on such a vehicle. Moreover, it is drawn not by horses but by two naked girls. In another scene the man and the woman are shown in what is known as the Geb-and-Nut position, he lying on the ground, she bowed over him. This could indicate a caricature of a religious representation. However, not all episodes can be explained as being allegorical.

Another question is whether the same man is throughout depicted. The figures show small differences, especially in the shape of the noses, but it is uncertain whether this is intentional. It is usually considered that the man who is here portrayed was elderly. He is partly bald, with unkempt hair on the back of his head, and he has a stubbly beard. In the first representations he is still vigorous, but later on his energy seems to have gone. He is seen lying under a bed on which the woman, clad merely in a girdle, is stretched out, leaning down to him and trying to seduce him (fig. 4). He appears to be exhausted, as the text, so far as it is legible, confirms. In the next scene the woman, assisted by two girls, carries him away. His phallus, still of enormous dimensions, is now flaccid.

Although it is not absolutely clear whether the bawdy representations deride an elderly person, that seems the most likely interpretation. Whether the story is thought to take place in Deir el-Medina is not certain; more likely the City itself (Thebes, on the east bank) was the location of the brothel. For our purposes it is significant that it is a caricature of a man of advanced years. In the next chapter we will encounter more dignified representations of elderly persons.

II The Aged in Art

The vast majority of Egyptian representations of men, whether in two or three dimensions, portrays them as healthy, vigorous, and comely; the body is muscular, with wide shoulders and a slender waist. In short, they are seen as ideal human beings. Although minor personal traits can occasionally be recognized, the images are no portraits in our sense of the word.

That is proved by those cases in which we happen to possess two statues of one and the same man. An example is the two wooden statues of the chancellor Nakhti, found in his Middle Kingdom tomb at Asyut. Discovered during the French excavations of 1893, they are now in the Cairo and Louvre Museums. If the inscriptions on their bases did not confirm that they represent the same man, then nobody would have surmised it, for their faces are totally different. That is, although Egyptian art has sometimes been provided with labels such as "realistic", or even "naturalistic", it does not attempt to reproduce reality as a photograph does.

It is against this background that we have to study those statues and reliefs or paintings that have been suggested to depict middle-aged or older men. The age does generally not so much appear from the face, but rather from the build of the figure, which is in some instances that of a corpulent, prosperous looking official. A well-known example is the Fifth Dynasty wooden statue known as the "Sheikh el-Beled" (see p. 70); another is the Fourth Dynasty limestone seated statue of Hemiunu, now in Hildesheim, whose adiposity reflects his successful lifestyle (see fig. 51).

Whether these persons should be called "elderly" is mainly a matter of definition. In view of the low life expectancy in those days (see pp. 31-34), men of over forty, the age at which they reached the pinnacle of their career, were certainly considered to be "young old" (see p. 1), and that is what their statues are intended to show.

In contrast to men, representations of elderly women are rare. Statues of them are restricted to a few figures of women grinding grain. Generally, it is only from the lower levels of society that women are shown to be old, and they are never depicted as being overweight. The only fat lady in Egyptian art is the famous Ati, the obese wife of the chief of Punt, pictured on the walls of Queen Hatshepsut's mortuary temple at Deir el-Bahri. However, she was a foreigner. The Egyptians clearly considered her figure to be an object of ridicule, as is aptly demonstrated by a lively drawing on a Ramesside ostracon, obviously intended as a caricature.

Male corpulence is not the only sign of advanced age. Others are bending over and leaning on a stick (see Chapter 7), stress on a fat upper torso, even to the extent of what look like pendulous breasts, grey hair, and baldness. The latter characteristic can almost only be seen in representations of workmen, for the upper classes hid it under a wig! If the élite are shown bald, it is not a sign of old age but of belonging to the priesthood. Of course, grey, or even white hair, can only be seen in paintings, which are none too frequent. We will return to this point at the end of the chapter.

In some Old Kingdom mastabas the owner appears on the walls in two different guises: once as a slender, youthful man, and once as an older, corpulent personality. An example can be found in the Saqqara tomb of a certain Khabausokar, called Hethes, which is dated to the Third or early Fourth Dynasty. On both sides of the entrance is a niche where the owner is depicted as a rather obese individual, with a staff in his hand and wearing an elaborate necklace. In a Fifth Dynasty mastaba at Giza, of a certain Rakhaefankh, the owner appears at both sides of the doorway. Left he is represented as an ideal, slender adult, and right as an elderly man with a fat breast and belly. In the Sixth Dynasty tomb of the vizier Khentika, called Ikhekhi, also at Saqqara, so well published by the former Keeper of the Egyptian Department at the British Museum,

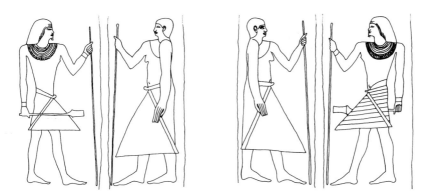

Two figures of Khentika on both sides of the entrance doorway of his tomb (Mastaba of Khentika at Saqqara, Sixth Dynasty). (Fig. 5)

T.G.H. James, we see the high official in the doorway on both sides depicted twice (fig. 5). He walks into the tomb as a slender adult, whereas on the thickness he walks outwards as a beardless older man, wearing a long kilt and displaying rolls of fat along his body. It has been suggested that the latter picture presents Khentika after his retirement, the other in his prime when he held office.

Stout elderly gentlemen also occasionally occur in other Old Kingdom tombs. East of the smaller pyramids that belong to the Great Pyramid of Khufu (Cheops) at Giza, in the so-called East Field, the mastaba of Queen Merysankh III is situated. She was the wife of the Pharaoh Khafra (Chephren) and the daughter of Kawab, Khufu's eldest son. In the offering chamber her father is once depicted, in accordance with his age as a heavily built man.

Another such obese person is represented in the mastaba of Seshemnefer IV, in the Central Field of Giza, South of the causeway of Chephren, reliefs of which are now in Hildesheim. The tomb dates from the late Fifth to early Sixth Dynasty. However, this is a picture of a statue, not of a living person, as appears evident from the accompanying caption. Priests are depicted bringing offerings to it.

Also in Hildesheim there is a wooden seated statue of the Sixth Dynasty, belonging to a certain Hetepi, which came from his tomb in the West Field of Giza. The posture is exceptional: the back slightly bent, the head bowed somewhat forward. Such an attitude occurs with statues of squatting scribes, but that is not the case here. It has been suggested that it is an expression of Hetepi's advanced age. If that is a correct interpretation, it seems to be a unique case.

The final example of a dignitary that we mention from the Old Kingdom occurs in the Sixth Dynasty mastaba of Nefer and his father Kahay, situated at Saqqara, South of the Djoser compound, and nearby the causeway of Unas. On one wall the father is shown as a distinctly corpulent individual, leaning on a stick, whereas on the false door he appears, like Nefer himself everywhere in the tomb, in the traditional slender posture.

In all these cases the persons represented as elderly belong to the élite, whether they are tomb-owners or members of their family. But the walls of the mastabas also bear scenes which show us aged servants. An example is the Sixth Dynasty tomb of Kaemankh, again situated in the West Field of Giza. Two people are depicted preparing bread, one of whom is a naked, bald man with a conspicuously square skull, a short unkempt beard, and a rather fat body. He kneads the batter in a dish for the round loaves his younger workmate, in the register above, is patting into shape.

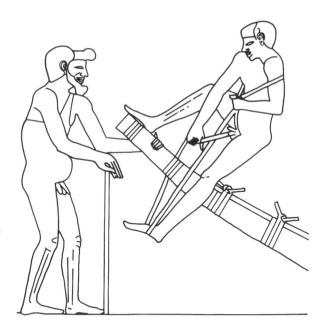

A naked pot-bellied old man chats to a ship-wright (Tomb of Ukhhotep at Meir, Twelfth Dynasty). (Fig. 6)

Two other figures, equally naked and corpulent, with stubble beards, are shown building a papyrus boat in the famous mastaba of Ti at Saqqara, which dates from the Fifth Dynasty. Yet another man occurs on a wall from the tomb of a certain Persen at Saqqara. This relief is now in the Bode-Museum in Berlin. He exhibits a deeply lined face and a rather swollen body, and is busily engaged in carrying a yoke laden with offerings.

Not only men from the lower levels of society show in some cases signs of their advanced years. In the tomb chapel of a Pepinakht, called Heni the Black, at Meir, of the Sixth Dynasty, there is in a corner a depiction of a squatting man. According to the caption, he was inspector of the prophets, treasurer of the god, scribe of the nome, and superintendent of the scribes, and bore the name of Ankhy. These copious titles imply that he was a middle ranking provincial official. Certainly, the corpulence of Ankhy's body indicates that he was accustomed to lead a quiet, sedentary life!

Proceeding to the Middle Kingdom, another tomb at Meir, namely that of the nomarch (provincial governor) Ukhhotep, son of Senbi, of the Twelfth Dynasty, also contains pictures of some corpulent officials. Two of them are shown standing behind the tomb-owner and his wife, rolls of fat on their bodies indicating that they had attained a comfortable

Painted limestone relief of an anonymous aged official with a close-up of the face (?Saqqara, transitional Eighteenth/Nineteenth Dynasty). (Fig. 7)

position. A similar figure can be seen standing behind the seated Ukhhotep, while on another wall a stout herald is depicted walking behind two long-horned oxen. A meagre cowherd with spindly legs and a long, round beard conducts the animals to his master. The contrast between the herdsman, shuffling along and supporting his tottering steps on a short, knobby stick, and the prosperous, well-fed official is striking. Of course, adiposity is in itself no definite proof of advanced age, no more than the meagreness of the cowherd is sufficient to characterize

18

him as elderly. Yet, the contrast is certainly intentional, representing two aspects of old age, one of the poor, the other of those who are well-off.

In the same tomb another elderly man is depicted. Leaning on his stick, he is standing before a boat on which shipwrights are busy binding bundles of papyrus with ropes (fig. 6). The naked fellow, pot-bellied, with a shock of hair over his forehead and a rather long beard, chats away to the workmen, doubtless uttering all kinds of platitudes. This is obviously a caricature of old age, but certainly a fine one.

With the stela of the singer Neferhotep, now in Leiden, we enter quite a different sphere. Actually, there exist two pictures of this musician. The other occurs on a stela of his master, also in Leiden, where he is playing the harp for Iki and his wife. Above the head of the obese, bald Neferhotep a brief song is written. It runs:

> O Tomb, you have been built for a feast,
> you have been founded for goodliness.

This is a typical harper's song of the Middle Kingdom, a composition addressed to the tomb, not to the deceased.

On the other stela the singer also appears as an obese, elderly man. It was devoted to his memory after his death by two friends, a carrier of bricks and a draughtsman who were responsible for its rather mediocre execution. Probably Neferhotep had no relatives, so that his comrades, simple people like himself, performed for him the last rites. His marked adiposity may be due to his sedentary lifestyle. In other instances a corpulent harpist is sometimes depicted as being blind (see fig. 23), which would explain the lack of mobility.

Before turning to the New Kingdom a few words should be said about some statues of Twelfth Dynasty Pharaohs, particularly those of Sesostris III. The heads of these, at least from his later years, have been interpreted as being those of an elderly man, disappointed by life. In their traits, scholars have wanted to see world-weariness, pensive melancholy, and suchlike. This has even been connected with the events of his reign, and thought to be reflected in the literature of that age. Certainly, the artistic style shows profound changes during the reign of this Pharaoh, but whether they reflect his psychological reactions is questionable. It is also not even clear whether these statues represent Sesostris as an elderly man. If so, then it is only his face, for the body also exhibits the traditional slender, youthful figure.

Perhaps the most expressive portrait of a man of advanced years in all Egyptian art is the relief on a limestone block from a tomb, probably at Saqqara, and now in the Brooklyn Museum, New York (fig. 7). On account of its style it can be dated without hesitation to the post-Amarna Period. With his furrowed forehead, the deep line from the nostril to the corner of the mouth, the flabby double chin and the prominent Adam's apple, this unknown personality provides us with a model of the Egyptian view of dignified old age. Note should also be taken of the protruding collar bone, as well as of his skinny wrists and bony fingers. In how far it is a reliable portrait we cannot know, but it is without doubt the most striking expression of the subject of this book.

Not much less powerful is the head of the black granite kneeling statue of Amenhotep, son of Hapu (see pp. 61, 76, and 130), from the time of Amenhotep III. Found at Karnak in 1901, in front of the Seventh Pylon, it exhibits the characteristics of an old man: hollow cheeks, deep grooves from nose to chin, and a meagre neck. That the body clearly expresses old age cannot be said. The inscription, however, tells us that Amenhotep was already eighty years of age. Yet, it has recently been argued that the sculpture was actually usurped from a Twelfth Dynasty statue, with a few minor retouches. On the other hand, a second scholar has rejected this suggestion, considering it to be a genuine Eighteenth Dynasty work of art. This controversy indicates just how difficult it can be to interpret and date Egyptian statuary.

A third piece derives from a house in the North Suburb of el-Amarna, where it was found during the British excavations of 1928-29; it is now in the Cairo Museum. An 18 centimetres high, painted limestone statuette of a man seated on a chair, it is a remarkable example of the art of the period. The toothless mouth, gaunt neck, the grooves from the nostrils downwards, the prominent collar bones, all these traits strongly suggest an elderly man. Corpulence, on the other hand, is only discreetly suggested, as in the statue of Amenhotep, son of Hapu.

Of an earlier date is the picture of the Theban mayor Sennefer (see fig. 2). As we have stated (see p. 9), this is the only depiction in his tomb in which his age is indicated by rolls of fat. In all other instances he is portrayed in the traditional manner as a slender adult. That his advanced age is only delicately suggested, and does not appear in his face, is in accordance with the more restrained style of the Tuthmosid Period.

As for scenes with elderly workmen, we have already mentioned one from the tomb of Paheri at el-Kab (see fig. 3). Such representations are rather frequent in the New Kingdom. We will discuss a few of them.

Several persons of advanced age are depicted in the Theban tomb of Puyemre (TT 39), the Second Prophet of Amun in the time of Tuthmosis III. They are herdsmen and artisans, and their age is indicated by a bald forehead, in some cases with a tuft of hair in front,

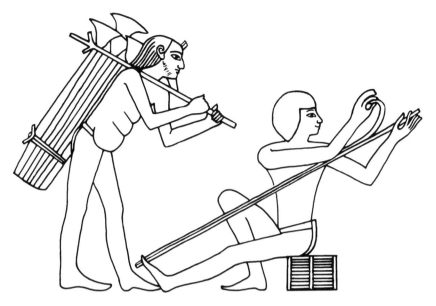

A naked elderly labourer carrying a bundle of papyrus stems (Tomb of Puyemre (TT 39), Eighteenth Dynasty). (Fig. 8)

while the remaining locks fall untidily to the nape of the neck. They also have a pointed beard, and exhibit a tendency to flabbiness. An example is a naked labourer carrying a large bundle of papyrus stems on his back, while his younger colleague sits and strips them (fig. 8).

A similar figure is the bent ploughman in the Theban tomb of Nakht (TT 52), of the time of Tuthmosis IV and Amenhotep III. On his thin legs he hobbles behind the team of oxen, trying to steer the plough. In the vintage scene in the same tomb two elderly men are depicted with grey hair and pot-bellies, one picking grapes and the other bending over the overflow from the wine-press.

Not only the élite and the simple workers occasionally show signs of being elderly. As in the Middle Kingdom, we also come across instances of lower officials. A fine example occurs in the Theban tomb of the Great Herald Antef (TT 155), again dating from the time of Hatshepsut and Tuthmosis III. As part of a series of vineyard scenes we see an overseer sitting on a mat in a pavilion, while a naked girl stands before him, offering him a cup of wine. He is a stout man, with an almost pendulous breast, and is designated as a manager by the staff in his hand. The scene is somewhat damaged, but the essential elements are recognizable. A

Black granite head of an elderly man (Temple of Mut at Karnak, Twenty-Fifth Dynnasty or ?Middle Kingdom). (Fig. 9)

caption gives the words spoken by the girl: "For your *ka*! Receive the good thing with the *ka* of the Herald Antef!" This rather stilted translator's English is rendered by the publisher of the tomb as: "To your health! Take this and drink to the health of the Herald Antef!" Whereupon the man, putting the cup to his lips, answers: "How sweet is the wine of the workers. To the *ka* of the Herald Antef as a gift from you, Renenutet."

Higher still on the social ladder brings us to a scene in the Theban tomb of the Overseer of the Treasury Dhuti (TT 11), which is also of the same period. Before the tomb-owner, who stands adoring Amen-Re, a smaller figure is shown, with rolls of fat on his breast like Sennefer (see fig. 2). This is very probably the father of the deceased. Herewith we are back to our point of departure, namely the top stratum of society. We can now move on to the Late Period.

Perhaps the most famous personality of that epoch is Montuemhat, Fourth Prophet of Amun, Mayor of Thebes, and Governor of Upper Egypt, who flourished at the end of the Twenty-Fifth Dynasty and at the beginning of the next one. Of him a number of statues are known, rendering him in the traditional manner. However, in 1897 a black granite sculpture was found during the excavations of Miss Margaret Benson in the Mut Temple at Karnak, portraying him as an elderly man. Now in Cairo, it is a broken fragment with only the head and shoulders remaining. Hence, one cannot say anything about the body, but the sagging facial muscles certainly suggest advanced age. The work is generally acknowledged as a masterpiece of Egyptian sculpture, although its identity as a representation of Montuemhat has been disputed.

To this statesman has also been ascribed a head, now in the Petrie Museum (fig. 9). Although it also provenances from the Mut Temple at Karnak, the attribution is far less certain. Doubtless it represents an old man with a heavily wrinkled face, but, as recently as 1991, it was suggested that the piece be redated to the Middle Kingdom. Again, this demonstrates the problems posed to us by Egyptian sculpture.

Clearly showing Montuemhat, since it provenances from his Theban tomb (TT 34), is a relief at present in Kansas City. Here he is portrayed offering to Anubis, and he exhibits the features of an ageing man: puffy eyes and sagging cheeks, as well as a bald skull. In almost all other representations from his tomb he displays the idealized traits of a youthful personality. It should be noted, however, that the usual adiposity of elderly men is here not indicated.

In the last centuries B.C. some instances occur of real portraiture, showing individuals as they will have looked in life. Whether that is due to foreign influence, Greek and later Roman, is a matter of discussion. We will here mention only one example. In Baltimore is the head of a statue described as the "Tired Old Man". Its realism is evident. The face displays the resignation, even the disappointment with life that we sometimes encounter in elderly people. Here we are far removed from the reserved manner in which Egyptian art in general exhibits the manifestations of old age.

As mentioned above, one of the means by which advanced age was indicated is grey, or even white hair. The instances are not very numerous because not too many paintings or reliefs have survived. Those we possess all seem to come from the New Kingdom, particularly from the tombs of the necropolis workmen at Deir el-Medina, and these are the ones that we will now cite.

A fine example occurs in the tomb of Pashedu (TT 3), from the Nineteenth Dynasty (fig. 10 and cover illustration). On a short wall beside the entrance to the burial chamber three registers with representations of Pashedu's relatives are to be found. In the top row his father, whose hair is completely white, and his mother, who is grey, are followed by his three brothers who are clearly younger. In the middle row we have first his father-in-law, with pepper-and-salt coloured hair, then his mother-in-law, who is grey. After her comes a lady whose place in the family is not quite clear, and whose black wig exhibits grey ends. The other women in this row, and Pashedu's children in the bottom register, are all too young for grey hair.

The relatives of the workman Pashedu and his wife. First register: his family; second register: her family; third register: their children (Tomb of Pashedu (TT 3), Nineteenth Dynasty). (Fig. 10)

In the tomb of the sculptor Ipuy (TT 217), also from the Nineteenth Dynasty and famous for its lively scenes, the deceased is once depicted while libating to the gods. The wall is slightly damaged, but it is clearly visible that Ipuy here has grey hair, whereas elsewhere in the tomb his hair is black.

The tomb of Irinefer (TT 290), another necropolis workman from the Ramesside Period, contains a picture of the deceased and his wife in which both are wearing white wigs. By contrast, on a stela from its chapel, now in Paris, where Irinefer and his wife are shown censing before his parents and brothers, it is his father Siwadjyt, who is white-haired.

There are also a few instances of grey hair from tombs outside of Deir el-Medina. In that of Puyemre cited above, which shows so many balding heads, one man is depicted whose hair at the back of his head is greying. He is busy gutting fish, and has a pointed beard, his forehead being hairless as is usual in this tomb.

Finally, we turn to the Theban tomb of the Viceroy of Kush Amenhotep, called Huy (TT 40), of the time of Tutankhamun (see p. 71). Here a scene occurs in which men and women bring to him the Nubian tribute. One of the men is partly bald, with a ring of hair around the base of his skull, while three of the women are shown with white hair. Below these people, in the middle register, an elderly woman is leaning upon a stick, whose hair is also white (see fig. 29).

The examples we have cited, and which can easily be supplemented, demonstrate that the Egyptians were by no means loath to show old age on their tomb-walls, especially not when persons from the lower strata of society were concerned. This was achieved by the shape of the body or by the colour of the hair. Facial traits indicating that the person represented was old are almost only found in statuary, which by its very nature means: representations of the upper class. The vast majority of two- or three-dimensional figures are shown, however, throughout Egyptian history, as vigorous, slender, youthful persons.

III Mummies and Medicine

The state of their body is for human beings at its optimum level between the ages of eighteen and thirty. In these years their growth is completed, biologically their organism has stabilized, their skills and reaction times are at their best. After this point, signs of decay begin to appear: reaction time increases, the lens of the eye begins to harden, the efficiency of oxygen transfer in the lungs begins to decline; blood pressure rises since the tissue in the arteries becomes less elastic. Strength and endurance, however, still remain fairly constant into the forties. By the fifth decade of life the signs of old age become more pronounced: blood pressure rises further, tissues becoming even less elastic, strength and endurance decline. In short, old age commences.

Is it possible to trace this development from the study of Egyptian mummies? Did the Egyptians themselves speak about it in their medical papyri? The short answer to these questions is simply: no!

During the last twenty years or so a large number of investigations into human remains, skeletons and mummies, have been published, executed with modern techniques such as radiography and blood-group analysis. However, the results have been until now rather disappointing from the Egyptological point of view. This is mainly because the scientific methods applied are not yet sufficiently advanced to produce the results which Egyptology requires. An example may serve to indicate what we mean. Investigations of his mummy have led to the conclusion that Tutankhamun was at his death between sixteen and twenty-five years old. However, that is precisely what the historical documents long ago suggested. What Egyptologists want to know is: what exactly was his age, sixteen or twenty-five years? That the scientists are not yet able to tell us.

The medical papyri, interesting as they are in showing us how advanced Pharaonic civilization was in this respect, do not explicitly deal with the problem of ageing. One of them is the Papyrus Ebers, named after its first modern owner, the German Egyptologist Georg Ebers, who purchased it in Luxor from Edwin Smith and published it in 1875. Ebers was Professor of Egyptology at Leipzig, where the papyrus is now housed in the University Library. He is also known as the author of some historical novels that take place in Ancient Egypt, including the famous *Eine ägyptische Königstochter* (1864), translated into English as *An Egyptian Princess*.

The papyrus named after him is no less than 20 metres long and is therefore one of the longest papyri that we possess. It dates from the early Eighteenth Dynasty and deals with all kinds of medical matters. Actually the text contains a number of monographs and excerpts devoted, among other subjects, to internal diseases and their treatment, to eye and skin disorders, to gynaecological topics, to heart and blood vessels, etc. It also contains a dozen prescriptions for the loss of hair. Since baldness is a common sign of getting old, this is pertinent to our subject.

Another medical text is the Papyrus Edwin Smith, named after the American dealer who acquired it, together with Papyrus Ebers, in 1862. It was presented by his daughter to the New York Historical Society and is now housed in the Academy of Medicine in New York. This surgical treatise is an Eighteenth Dynasty copy of an earlier original, and was published in 1930 by the great American Egyptologist James H. Breasted.

In an appendix, written in a different hand from the rest of the text, we find some prescriptions for ointments said to smooth an old, wrinkled skin when applied to it. They are processed from the legume fenugreek (*Trigonella faenum graecum*), which is washed, dried, cooked and ground. Actually, the paragraphs containing these prescriptions are called "Book for transforming an Old Man into a Youth", but that seems a little overdone. However, maybe the claims are no more outrageous than those associated with modern cosmetic surgery, in particular, some advertisements for a face lift.

All this is interesting, but only marginally connected with the problems of growing old. That life was a precarious matter in those days we have noted in the Introduction. A rise in life expectancy during our century from 44.1 (men) and 47.8 (women) years to 72.4 and 78.1 speaks volumes. What the figures were in the time of the pyramids, or even in that of Ramesses II, we do not know. It was only in the Late Period that the Egyptians in some instances noted the age of death, and that only of some more important persons.

The hardships of those ages are perhaps best illustrated by the report of a mining expedition to the Wadi Hammamat in year 3 of Ramesses IV (*circa* 1150 B.C.). Of the 9268 men, all certainly adults, no less than 900 are reported to have died. And this was a peaceful mission to acquire valuable building stone for Pharaoh's monuments. If this was supposed to be the norm, how large would the chance of reaching old age have been for the mass of the population?

Medical investigations of human remains have certainly taught us something about the health of the people. We know that all kinds of infections were a major cause of disease and mortality, that arteriosclerosis and arthritis made the life of elderly people difficult as in our days; that all manner of diseases, such as bilharzia (schistosomiasis), poliomyelitis, and tuberculosis rendered them victims. However, it is not possible from isolated cases found in some mummies to draw conclusions as to the frequency of these illnesses among the population as a whole.

One point seems to be certain, although it is historical evidence rather than the medical investigations that suggest it: the food situation seems generally to have been satisfactory. Famines did occur, but were not too frequent. The oldest representation we know of occurs along the pyramid causeway of the Pharaoh Unas at South Saqqara and can be dated to the end of the Fifth Dynasty. Here two rows of living skeletons are depicted, men and women and one child. They sit and lie down, exhausted by hunger. In the lower register we see an old bearded man, supported by his wife and son. Altogether this is a moving, realistic picture of what famine meant in those days.

Equally realistic, but less poignant, is the statuette of a potter, now in the Oriental Institute at Chicago (fig. 11). It forms part of a group of servant statuettes from the Fifth to Sixth Dynasty mastaba of Nikauinpu at Giza, the exact location of which is at present unknown. The undernourished craftsman, whose meagre back clearly shows his prominent ribs, squats before his wheel, while three of his pots stand ready beside him. Perhaps this piece refers to the same famine as the scene on the Unas causeway.

The worse period for the food supply may have been the First Intermediate Period and the succeeding Middle Kingdom. From that time we have many indications of low Nile inundations and famine. In how far this was really a major problem of those days, or whether it was to a certain extent a literary cliché is not certain. Anyhow, medical researches have not yet brought forward evidence that malnutrition was common, although we have to keep in mind that the mummified dead belonged to the upper echelons of society. The depictions of emaciated persons usually show bedouins from the desert. The influence of a lack of food on old age and mortality in Egyptian history is difficult to estimate, however.

At the end of the Twentieth Dynasty many tombs in the Theban necropolis fell victim to robbers. Several papyri (see p. 89) inform us about the investigations and trials of the plunderers. The royal tombs in the Valley of the Kings, however, seem to have escaped this desecration. They were indeed opened and systematically stripped of their contents,

Limestone statuette of an under-nourished potter squatting at his wheel (Mastaba of Nikauinpu at Giza, Fifth to Sixth Dynasty). (Fig. 11)

but at least partly on the order of the authorities, who used them as treasuries in these economically less prosperous days. The royal mummies were removed from their resting places, unwrapped in order to appropriate their jewellery, then rewrapped, and buried elsewhere. After some moves they ended up in two places, one high up in the cliffs behind Deir el-Bahri (generally known as the tomb of Inhapi), others in a side-room in the tomb of Amenhotep II in the Valley of the Kings (KV 35).

At the end of the last century these caches were discovered, the tomb of Inhapi in 1871 by the local Abd el-Rasul family, that of Amenhotep II by the French excavator Victor Loret in 1898. The mortal remains of almost all the New Kingdom Pharaohs were brought to Cairo, where they are now on display in the Egyptian Museum. In the following years they were examined by the Australian anatomist Grafton Elliot Smith, and in 1966-73 again, this time by an American team from the University of Michigan using modern methods including radiology.

One would expect that the latter project would have provided us with the answers to several questions, particularly that of the age of death of these rulers, but, unfortunately, that is hardly the case. The subject was studied back in the United States from the X-ray films, but the results are generally far too low. Ramesses II, for example, was stated to have died

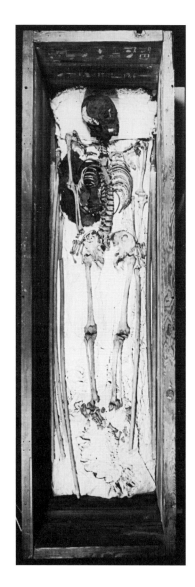

*Skeleton of Idu II lying in
his cedar coffin (Mastaba
of Idu II at Giza, Sixth
Dynasty). (Fig. 12)*

at fifty to fifty-five years of age, whereas we know that he reigned until his sixty-seventh regnal year. That he would have ascended the throne more than ten years before his birth seems unlikely. Amenhotep III, to quote another example, who celebrated three *sed*-festivals (see Chapter 11), the last in his thirty-eighth regnal year, was calculated to have lived until his thirty-ninth year. Admittedly, the physicians who suggested these ages meant them to be minima, but they are so far out of the known range that they are useless.

There is yet another problem with the royal mummies. Those who re-wrapped them and wrote on the new bandages the names of the Pharaohs seem to have made mistakes. Moreover, when they arrived in Cairo the labelling was not carried out very carefully. Thus, in several cases, there is serious doubt about the real identity.

So it appears evident that the royal mummies, despite the work carried out on them, have not advanced our knowledge concerning the age of death. That some Pharaohs died at an advanced age we know from historical evidence (see Chapter 11), but not from the study of their mortal remains.

For a better insight into the causes and age of decease we need not so much the study of a single individual, although that will sometimes reveal interesting details, but of large groups, by preference from one period and one site as well as from the same social stratum. For instance, in the museum in Hildesheim is preserved the skeleton of a certain Idu II, a high official of the Sixth Dynasty whose mastaba was found in 1914 in the West Field of Giza. The body was lying in a sumptuous cedar coffin, in which were also some objects including seven walking sticks (see Chapter 7), and two large bundles of "clothing" resting by his feet. All these are housed in the same museum and in 1987 an investigative project took place there. One of us was invited to unwrap the "clothing" and discovered instead twelve linen sheets. At the same time the human remains (fig. 12) were the subject of an extensive palaeopathological study, as a result of which we know that this Idu was a healthy man all his life, although he suffered from chronic inflammation of the middle ear. When he died he was between fifty-five and sixty-five years old. Interesting as all this is, it does not teach us much about old age in Ancient Egypt in general.

For determining the age of death two criteria are used: the pattern of tooth formation, and that of ossification. On account of these three mummies in the Philadelphia University Museum (called PUM II, III, and IV) could be established to have died at 35 to 40 years, at 42 years, and at 8 to 10 years respectively. Again, for our present subject not so very important.

Somewhat more information resulted from an investigation carried out during the seventies of almost a hundred individuals in various collections in the former Czechoslovakia. Among them were 53 complete human remains, 7 of them 20 to 30 years old, 13 of 30 to 40 years, 6 of 40 to 50 years, 11 of 50 to 60 years, and 8 of even over 60 years. The total is 45, while 8 were classified as juveniles of under 20 years.

This can be compared with the results of a study of the mummies in the British Museum conducted in the sixties. Of the 35 for which the age could be established, 11 were between 40 and 50 years old, and 9 were even older. While for the Czechoslovakian bodies the average age of the men was 43.7 years, and of the women 41.3, that of the London ones was also between 40 and 45. What is conspicuous is the relatively large group of the over fifties, more than one would expect. However, this is not a random sample taken from the entire population. The percentage of young persons, particularly babies and infants, is far too low. They were usually not buried in the main cemeteries; in some cases they were even laid to rest under the floor of the houses.

Although these particular studies are a good example of what can be done, we have to keep in mind that these mummies provenance from a large number of sites, mostly unknown, and from all periods of Egyptian history. They also tend to belong to the higher classes of society. Poor people were not extensively mummified, that was far too expensive. That among the 45 adults in the Czechoslovakian group no less than 11 came from the workmen's village at Deir el-Medina (see p. 9) is not contradictory to this statement, for these artisans belonged to the best paid people of their time.

Extremely important for our knowledge of the palaeodemography of Egypt was the investigation of approximately 850 individuals from one Predynastic cemetery at Naga ed-Deir. This site, south of Akhmim, was excavated in 1902-03 by the American expedition of George Reisner and Albert Lythgoe, which opened 635 tombs. All contained typical burials of that early period: the bodies, lying on their left side, were in a flexed position. Although the cemetery had already been plundered in Predynastic times, and also disturbed in later ages, the results of this meticulous publication are truly impressive.

The excavators were not only able to establish the sex of most of the bodies, but also the age, and incidentally even the cause of death. Examples are Tomb N 7140 (fig. 13a), a woman of between fifty and sixty years old, whose rump was perfectly preserved because it was covered by a large dish, and Tomb N 7081 (fig. 13b), an elderly woman with long, wavy, greying hair, who probably died from chronic constipation.

From a total of 265 persons, comprising 182 sub-adults and 83 adults, the age of 67 individuals could be established as follows: 11 of between 20 and 30 years, 27 of 30 to 40 years, 15 of 40 to 50 years, and 14 of over 50 years, of whom one was even over 60. Clearly, infant and child mortality were high, at 182 out of 265; even more than the figures indicate, because of the habit of burying infants in the houses. The

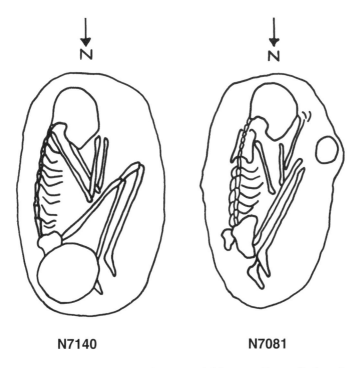

Skeletons of elderly women, each accompanied by a pot (from a Predynastic Cemetery at Naga ed-Deir: (a) Tomb N 7140; (b) Tomb N 7081). (Fig. 13)

relatively high mortality between 30 and 35 (16 individuals) was of course due to occupational hazards and the risk of childbirth. If one survived this, disease and the factors associated with getting older began to take their toll. Yet, a relatively large proportion of the population (*circa* 10 per cent) appear to have survived into their fifties.

Another investigation, undertaken in the seventies, was that of the large mummy collection in the Anthropological Institute in Turin, partly from the Predynastic and partly from the Dynastic Period, which derived from excavations conducted at Gebelein and Asyut between 1911 and 1935. The average age of the latter group turned out to be 36 years, that of the former only 30 years, so substantially lower than those of the Czechoslovakian and the British Museum investigations. That was caused by a larger proportion of juveniles. The mortality among young adults was very high. At 43 years only a quarter of the Dynastic group was still alive, whereas the Predynastic one had already been reduced to a quarter at 30 years. As is to be expected, the mortality of women up to

30 years was higher than that of men, while later the pattern was reversed. Of the 876 people investigated, 215 had died between the ages of 40 and 60 (24.5 per cent), while only 16 (1.8 per cent) managed to survive beyond 60. On the other hand, 497 (54.5 per cent) had died between 20 and 40 years of age.

One of the most important groups of human remains to have been found in regular excavations derives from the mastabas of the West Field of Giza. One batch of these was discovered between 1911-13 by the German excavator Hermann Junker and consists of 177 skulls, all from the reign of Khufu (*circa* 2620 B.C.) and all belonging to the élite of that time. The collection is now in the Naturhistorisches Museum in Vienna, where it was studied in 1978 by the British dentist Filce Leek. For 50 individuals insufficient data could be collected, while for 27 even the sex remained uncertain. On the other hand, 28 persons were clearly over 40 years at the time of death, representing 17 men and 10 women (1 ambiguous).

Filce Leek also examined a second group of crania from the same cemetery, found by George Reisner in the same period. They had been housed ever since in a storeroom near the Giza Pyramids and were in a bad condition. Of the 62 items, selected at random, only 4 turned out to be over 40 years at death, all these being women. Such numbers are, however, too small to be representative.

The chronologically latest group we will mention derives from 25 tombs, dating from the Seventeenth and Eighteenth Dynasties, excavated in 1934-35 on the Western slope of the Qurnet Murai, East of Deir el-Medina. Some of these tombs contained more than one skeleton. Most of the human remains belonged to girls and young women, but there were also some elderly people. Proper medical research was not carried out on them in those years before the Second World War. Generally, the criterion of the excavator Bernard Bruyère when calling an individual "old" was based on the colour of the hair. One tomb contained a man and a woman, both of whom were grey; two others each housed a "very old man" with white hair. One other "very old man" was bald. It is clear that such statements are not really illustrative for our subject, the normal age of death of the entire population.

That is also not the case with a recent, highly sophisticated investigation. In 1986 the tomb of Maya was (re)discovered by a joint Egypt Exploration Society and Leiden Museum expedition working at South Saqqara. Scattered throughout the rooms and corridors of the lower level, the remains of five individuals were found, evidently those of Maya and his family. Careful reconstruction by an anthropologist has led to the following results. One, fairly robust man, was discovered to have been over fifty years of age; he could be identified as Maya himself, the Treasurer of Tutankhamun. A second man, probably just over forty, could have been Maya's brother, while a sturdy woman of medium height and over fifty years of age was probably his stepmother. Maya's wife Meryt appeared to be a slender lady of between twenty and forty years. The fifth mummy was that of a young teenager, thirteen to fourteen years old.

The investigations here described constitute merely a selection from all the modern researches into the medical aspects of the Ancient Egyptians. It is clear that, until now, the results for our problem, namely causes and age of death, are not overwhelming. A great deal more needs to be done before we reach satisfactory answers to these questions.

IV Households and Inheritance

The position of the aged in a particular society depends to a large extent on their ties with their descendants and relatives, that is, cognates (bilateral kinsmen and kinswomen) as well as affines (relatives by marriage). Hence, much is determined by the kinship structure of the society.

It is common knowledge that many peoples all over the world exhibit strong descent groups, a subject that is widely studied by social anthropologists. The descent may be patrilineal or matrilineal; seldom is it bilineal. Such groups possess all kinds of properties and privileges, and are usually exogamous.

However, strong kinship loyalties run against the demands of a bureaucratic state, and that Ancient Egypt certainly was from the early Old Kingdom onwards. No wonder therefore that we have never found in this civilization any traces of such powerful descent groups. Of course, the Egyptians acknowledged the importance of the family, members of the father's and of the mother's side being principally equal. They also recognized their connections with their affines, as appears clear from the representation of the relatives of a man's wife on stelae and in tombs. In this respect their society was similar to ours. But there were no rights vested in such kinship groups, no more than in our world.

A specific aspect worth mentioning is that, so far as we know, there existed no obligation to marry a particular relative, for instance, a father's or a mother's brother's daughter, as is found in many societies. The choice of a marriage partner seems to have been entirely free. It has been suggested that there was a preference for a paternal cross-cousin, but the proof for this is very weak. Of course, particularly when big financial and political interests were involved, the parents and the wider family pressed the young people to make a particular match. That happens also in our world.

As there were no strong descent groups with their own rights and resources as the basic units of Egyptian society, the main circle in which the elderly moved would have been their domestic group. In other words, those people who occupy or centre in a common dwelling, sharing many activities such as eating and child rearing, exercising control over family properties, etc. Such a household can be larger than the elementary family of parents and children; it may include unmarried siblings, brothers and sisters, uncles and aunts, as well as the parents or even the grandparents of both spouses, plus other elementary units of the second generation, and eventually servants.

A household ideally passes in the course of the years through a developmental cycle. Beginning with a couple, it grows when children are born. Then these children marry and a third generation enters, unless the custom is, as with us, that newly married people set up their own domestic unit: the so-called neo-local marriage. In this phase the household of the parents gradually decreases, until it ends as it started with just two people. Clearly, this scheme knows numerous variations. For instance, one of the children may at his or her wedding not leave the household but stay as a new elementary unit, forming part of the original domestic group. It may be the eldest son, but it is also sometimes the youngest, and, if there is no son, a daughter with her husband may act as heiress. Every reader can imagine such variations.

Moreover, the lines of division between the aspects of a household are not clear, as we shall see in the following pages. Its members may live under separate roofs, though near enough to each other to form a unit, or under one roof, but eating in each conjugal group. Yet they will generally socialize the children together, and sometimes work together in a common field. The question as to whether these are still domestic groups seems largely a matter of definition.

Turning to the Ancient Egyptian reality, we must state from the outset that of this subject remarkably little is known. It simply did not draw the attention of scholars. What we see resembles so much the world in which we live that it hardly seemed worthy of comment. That may well be a mistake. Admittedly, we possess minimal direct evidence on the domestic group, and it is difficult to establish whether what we have is typical or exceptional. Statistical material, so essential for the study of the household, is completely absent. Therefore we can do no better than to present some specific cases.

Among the Middle Kingdom papyri discovered in 1888-89 by Flinders Petrie in the settlement of Kahun in the Faiyum there are parts of a census list. This important document is now in the Petrie Museum and was published by F. Ll. Griffith in 1898. By chance the entries mention one household at successive stages of its developmental cycle, separated from each other by several years.

The earliest entry of the 'household list' records:

> The soldier, Dhuti's son Hori;
> his wife, Satsopdu's daughter Shepset;
> their son Snefru (according to a hieratic sign, a
> newborn baby).

This is obviously the first stage, a small elementary or nuclear family. The second entry shows significant additions to the household, recording:

> The soldier, Dhuti's son Hori;
> his wife, Satsopdu's daughter Shepset;
> their son Snefru (now designated with the sign for 'child');
> Hori's mother Harekhni;
> her daughters Qatsennut, Mekten, Ese, Rudet, and Satsnefru
> (of whom the last two are also designated as 'child').

Evidently, Hori's mother had come to live in the household, together with her five daughters, the youngest two of whom were still children. Probably this happened after the death of her husband Dhuti. We may also conclude that Hori was her eldest child, for her younger daughters belonged to the same age-group as her grandson Snefru.

A third entry (fig. 14) is said to be a copy of a houselist, dated to year 3 of King Sekhemkare, that is, Amenemhat V, of the early Thirteenth Dynasty. Fundamental changes in the composition of the household have taken place. Its head was now:

> The soldier, Hori's son Snefru.

Probably Hori had died, and Snefru had succeeded him, also as a military man. Yet, he seems still to have been young, no wife of his being mentioned. The household further comprised:

> His (Snefru's) mother, Satsopdu's daughter Shepset;
> his father's mother (Snefru's grandmother) Harekhni;
> his father's sisters (Snefru's aunts) Ese and Satsnefru.

The latter was, as we have seen, of approximately the same age as Snefru, although genealogically of an older generation.

A note is appended to the effect that these last three females had entered the household of Snefru's father in a year 2, which can hardly be that of Amenemhat V. For this the changes are too radical. Not only is there the fact that Hori has since disappeared, but it is also clear that three of his sisters have left the domestic unit, probably because they

The third entry of the houselist when Snefru was head of the family (Kahun, Thirteenth Dynasty). (Fig.14)

married. Even the last-but-youngest, Rudet, who was in the earlier entry still a child, is not there any more. Only the very youngest and one of her older sisters still belong to the household.

This text presents us with an exceptional insight into an Egyptian household during the Middle Kingdom. Commencing from Hori's nuclear family, it comprised at a certain moment three generations.

Perhaps this situation will not have lasted too long, for Harekhni may well have been relatively old according to Egyptian standards. Another change to be expected is the departure of the last two girls by marriage. On the other hand, one might anticipate that Snefru would soon find a wife and start his own nuclear family.

The entries mention only this one son, so that they do not reveal whether sons other than the eldest were accustomed to remain in the household. The daughters clearly married out. However, it is quite uncertain whether this single case can allow us to draw conclusions in general. Regrettably, other census lists are at present still unpublished, some from the New Kingdom workmen's community at Deir el-Medina having also survived.

Hori and his son Snefru were soldiers, hence relatively simple people. More important was Heqanakhte, a well-off landowner at the beginning of the Twelfth Dynasty. Eight of his papers were found by Herbert Winlock in 1921-22 in the passage of the tomb of Meseh, situated at the North side of the bay of Deir el-Bahri. They were lying in the rubble with which the floor had been levelled. How the documents ended up there we will never know, but they were evidently conceived of as being of no value and had therefore been discarded. For us, however, these records constitute an extremely valuable source of information for the period.

Four of the papyri bear letters, the remaining four accounts. For the present subject letter II is the most important. It is addressed by Heqanakhte to his mother and a lady who was perhaps his aunt, and further to his entire household. He speaks, among other matters, about the famine raging in the country, alluding even to cases of cannibalism, although that may well be exaggerated. In this connection Heqanakhte writes down the quantities of grain that he has allotted to each of the members of his household, and thus we know the composition of this domestic unit.

The household consisted of: Ipi, Heqanakhte's mother, together with her maid; Hetepet, perhaps his aunt, plus her maid; a certain Nakhte, son of Heti, a senior servant and Heqanakhte's agent, together with his family; Merisu, the eldest son, also with his own family; Sihathor, the second son, and Sinebut, the third one, both clearly still unmarried. There were also two younger sons, Anpu and Snefru, probably still teenagers; a woman called Siinut, who may be a daughter; May's daughter Hetepet, whose relation to the others is unknown; and two girls, Nofret and Sitweret, probably also daughters of Heqanakhte. From elsewhere in the correspondence we know that a woman called Iutemhab also lived in the house. She is designated with a word that Egyptologists used to translate as 'concubine'. Perhaps she was Heqanakhte's second wife. In how far her position was legal is a moot point. It should be noted, however, that the mother of Heqanakhte's sons and daughters, his first wife, is nowhere mentioned. She seems to have been deceased. Finally, there was a housemaid called Senen, who in Heqanakhte's eyes had behaved badly to Iutenhab, and whom he orders to be turned out of the house.

All together this is a large domestic group, comprising four generations: a mother and an aunt(?), Heqanakhte himself with a second wife, and several of his sons and daughters, the eldest son with his own family. To this there came some female servants, and the agent with his family as a separate nuclear unit. The entire household will have comprised some twenty or more persons.

But was this really a household? Above we hinted at the difficulties of applying strict criteria. These people may not have eaten together, for they each received their own grain rations. They may even have lived under separate roofs. On the other hand, it is clear from the correspondence and the accounts that they worked on and were responsible for Heqanakhte's estate, his fields and his cattle. In this respect they constituted a unit, in which the two elderly ladies, Ipi and Hetepet, found their place, each with her own maid.

An interesting point is the position of the woman whom we have called Heqanahkte's 'second wife'. He is very anxious that she should be treated well by the family, not only by the servant Senen. Of course, the rôle of a, possibly young, second wife in such a large household is never an easy one. The earlier translation 'concubine' suggests that she was not even regularly married to the head of the family, but that may well be a mistake. One has to keep in mind that, so far as we know, there existed in Ancient Egypt no formal sanction on a marriage in the form of a wedding ceremony. All such unions seem to have been 'common law' marriages. In this respect the position of a second wife was no lower than that of a first one. Even so, the opposition of her stepchildren could have made her life very unpleasant.

There is yet a third source for the study of the domestic unit in Egypt. This is of a totally different nature, namely the ground plan of el-Amarna, the city of Akhenaten and Nefertiti. Few settlements in Egypt have been excavated over a larger area, and the best known, namely Kahun from the Middle Kingdom and Deir el-Medina from the New Kingdom, are artificial constructions, created by the contemporary government. Of the main cities it is only el-Amarna of which a considerable portion has been uncovered, sufficient to convey an impression of how its inhabitants lived. There is, moreover, ample reason to believe that life in other New Kingdom cities was not noticeably different.

In 1980 the Swiss architect Herbert Ricke published the results of the excavations at el-Amarna by the German archaeologist Ludwig Borchardt. These had been conducted South of the central temple area in the years just before the outbreak of the First World War. On the splendid plans that accompany this impressive publication we can easily recognize, spread over this entire Southern zone, some large mansions within their compounds. They possess granaries, storerooms, and stables, as well as gardens, in which a chapel for the god Aton had sometimes been erected. In several cases it is possible to distinguish, within its surrounding walls, a second, smaller edifice, which it has been suggested was inhabited by a son and his family. Unfortunately, as the excavations of el-Amarna have produced only a few texts, this hypothesis cannot be proved. The property could as well be that of a steward or agent such as Heqanakhte's assistant Nakhte.

A second type of house, smaller than the main mansions and lacking the extensive outbuildings, but similarly well-constructed and consisting of several rooms, will have been inhabited by what we could term the middle class. These structures are also found in every quarter of the city. A separate upper or middle class district simply did not exist.

Around and between these two types of residences we find wards or clusters of relatively small, cheaply constructed buildings. These display thinner walls and, generally, fewer rooms. Two such simple house groups are here depicted (fig. 15). They are situated West of one of the main thoroughfares, the so-called High Priest Road, named after the mansion of Pawah, a High Priest of Aton, which is situated opposite the block on the East side of the road. Our example comprises two groups, one of four and one of three dwellings, here designated as Group A and Group B. They were not built at one time, but rather after each other in the course of the years, the later edifices filling in the gaps between the earlier ones.

That is clear in Group A. At its South side there is a relatively well-built and roomy property (here indicated as house (c)). It has thick walls, seven rooms, stairs to the roof, and an adjacent garden, probably for vegetables, of which the square plots were still visible during the excavations. This seems to be the earliest structure of the group. Somewhat later house (a) was built, with only five rooms plus the stairs, and the entrance at the narrow alley between the ward and the edifices to the North. Beside the entrance there are two additional rooms, perhaps to be identified as workshops. Between the houses (c) and (a), a small, lengthy dwelling was later inserted (b), with its entrance at its East side, from which the alley could be reached via a court. The fourth and newest house (d), situated beside (b) and its court, is very basic, with five small rooms and thin, rather oblique walls.

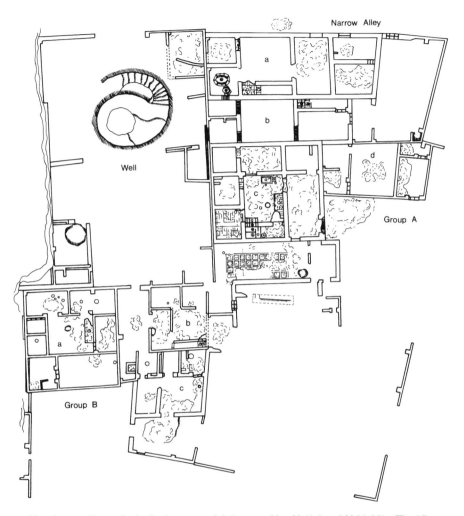

Two clusters of houses in the Southern zone of el-Amarna (Nos. N 49.9 and N 50.29). (Fig. 15)

The entire group lies adjacent to a wide courtyard in the West, where a common well was located. This served the inhabitants of several clusters – those further to the West (a sector excavated by the British in 1921-22), as well as our Group B. The latter consists of three, rather poor dwellings. The earliest and best is house (a), which is fairly regularly constructed and has eight rooms. House (b), however, is very small. Between (a) and (b) there was a narrow courtyard, with a stable at its inner end for a donkey, the brickwork trough for which is visible on the

Group of elderly men sitting in the shade (West Bank of Luxor, 1996). (Fig. 16)

plan. The third and latest house (c) has awkward oblique-angled walls. Three of them are solid, but at the North side it shares a thin partition wall with house (b).

What conclusions can we draw from this plan for the relations between the inhabitants of the wards? It is clear that they were closely connected, but that does not mean that they formed a single household. Each family lived under its own roof, and probably ate on its own. Yet, it seems probable that the later arrivals were in some way related to those who built the first houses. The whole situation in these clusters is one which still occurs in Modern Egypt, and many a tourist will have witnessed the picture. One can easily imagine the noise, the smell, and the dirt. The shouting children—whose socialization is more or less a duty of the entire community—and the elderly men sitting somewhere in the shade (fig. 16). It is in such surroundings that we have to picture the life of the elderly in Ancient Egypt in so far as they were not rich. That is, the majority of the aged population.

In contrast, tombs and other monuments, such as stelae and statues, show us the ideal life of the upper ten. There too we find the parents depicted as, for instance, in many New Kingdom tombs. Surprisingly, the mothers appear somewhat more frequently than the fathers, particularly when their position promoted the career of their sons. This happened for instance with the nurses of the king. Yet, one would expect to find the father as often, for it was his office that a son habitually inherited. This is not always evident in the accompanying texts, for the father is mostly indicated as *sab*. The word used to be regarded as a designation for a man who lacked any other title and, by consequence, to be indicative of the fact that the son rose to his position on his own merits. Recently, however, it has been suggested that it means something like 'the revered one', expressing the respect of the son for his late father. It is certainly conspicuous that *sab* is never used by a father for his son, nor by a man for himself.

In fact numerous instances are known where sons succeeded their fathers in high offices. A few famous examples may here suffice. The Vizier User(amun) (owner of TT 61 and 131) succeeded his father Iahmose (see p. 75), while he in his turn handed over his post to his nephew Rekhmire (TT 100). Hence, three members of one family held this supreme appointment in direct succession. A second example is the Overseer of the Granary Menkheperresonb (TT 79), who received the position after his father Nakhtmin (TT 87). All these individuals are well-known as the owners of splendid tombs on the Theban West Bank.

Of course, it was not possible to directly hand over one's office to one's son. For this the consent of Pharaoh, that is, of the government, was needed. Yet, these cases, and there are many more, demonstrate the tendency towards heredity in such appointments. Officially that was not so. In the Eighteenth Dynasty *Instruction of Ani* we read:

> The scribe is chosen for his hand,
> his office has no children.

In reality, however, many high dignitaries succeeded their fathers, or even their grandfathers.

A famous example of the practice of inheriting from one's maternal grandfather occurs in the biographical inscription of the Khnumhotep family, a line of Twelfth Dynasty nomarchs (provincial governors). It is inscribed on the dado beneath the paintings in the rock-cut sepulchre of Khnumhotep (III) at Beni Hasan in Middle Egypt. This tomb (No. 3), by far the best at the site, is well-known, particularly on account of a lively scene of brightly clad Semitic bedouin with their donkeys.

In 222 short vertical lines the family history is related. It begins with Khnumhotep (I), who was appointed by Pharaoh Amenemhat I, hence at the beginning of the dynasty, to rule over Menat-Khufu, a kind of district on the East bank of the Nile opposite the 16th or Oryx nome (province). Menat-Khufu, literally "wet nurse of Cheops", was originally called Menat-Snefru, a domain already mentioned in the early Fourth Dynasty. It is supposed to be the place where Cheops was born. The Middle Kingdom rulers of the region controlled the Eastern Desert as far as the Red Sea.

Khnumhotep (I) became later on nomarch of the Oryx nome, while his eldest son Nakht succeeded him in Menat-Khufu. Another son, Amenemhat, became under Sesostris I the nomarch of the 16th nome in succession to his father, while a daughter called Beket married a certain Nehri, a high official of the royal residence. It is the son of this couple, named after his maternal grandfather Khnumhotep (II), who succeeded in year 19 of King Amenemhat II his uncle Nakht in Menat-Khufu. He greatly enhanced his power by marrying Kheti, the heiress of the nomarch of the 17th or Jackal nome. So their eldest son, also called Nakht, became the ruler of that province, succeeding his maternal grandfather, while a second son, Khnumhotep (III), ruled in Menat-Khufu. It is he who related the story in his tomb.

Although these successions must have been confirmed by the central government, they seem to have been almost self-evident. For the nomarchs of the Middle Kingdom we can more or less accept this situation, for they were princes rather than officials. In other cases, the automatic succession by a son or a grandson seems to us in general an objectionable practice. But for the élite in Ancient Egypt it was the ideal. In the so-called "appeal to the living", texts inscribed on stelae and tomb-walls and addressed to the passer-by, the owner urges the latter to pronounce an offering formula for him, referring to his wish "to hand over your functions to your children". These words are frequently found in Middle and New Kingdom inscriptions, demonstrating that the desire was conceived to be obvious.

In general, children inherited all the possessions of their parents. This applied to daughters as well as to sons, and was one of the main sources of an individual's wealth, the other two being one's own activities and the favour of Pharaoh. That is nicely expressed in the text on a stelephorous statue (holding a stela) now in Cairo. It belongs to a certain Nekhtefmut, a fourth prophet of Amun, who lived during the Twenty-Second Dynasty under Osorkon II. He says:

> To me belong the things of my father and my mother,
> and of the hard work of my hands.

The lower half of the Second Kamose stela depicting the Overseer of the Seal Neshi, the ancestor of Mose (Karnak, late Seventeenth Dynasty). (Fig. 17)

> The rest [comes] from the favour of the kings
> whom I served in my time,
> there being found no fault of mine.
> With them I did what I wanted.

What Nekhtefmut did was to already hand over during his lifetime part of his properties to his beloved daughter, probably in recognition of the fact that she had taken care of her parents in their old age. This would explicitly not be deducted from her share in the inheritance at a later date.

It was through inheritance that the riches of grandparents and parents were preserved by their descendants. In particular, fields, the major source of wealth in this agrarian society, could remain in the family for centuries. A striking example is found in the record of some lawsuits which a certain Mose inscribed on the walls of his tomb-chapel at Saqqara in the Nineteenth Dynasty. It is a long and complicated saga that began in the early Eighteenth Dynasty under Pharaoh Ahmose and continued until the reign of Ramesses II.

King Ahmose, the liberator of the country from the Hyksos, conferred upon his faithful servant Neshi as a reward for his services a piece of land, subsequently known as the Hunpet of Neshi. This Neshi is probably the same person as the overseer of the seal depicted at the bottom of the Second Kamose stela, now one of the treasures of the Luxor Museum (fig. 17). It is he who had been responsible for erecting this important monument.

In the reign of Horemhab the estate was owned by six heirs of Neshi, for whom a woman called Wernero acted as a trustee. Her sister Takharu now called upon the lawcourt to divide the lands between the co-heirs, but even after an appeal the decision was that the fields remained undivided. Wernero's son Huy finally received the actual possession of the estate, cultivating the fields year after year.

On his death the property came into the hands of his widow Nubnofret, but her rights were disputed by an administrator called Khay, of whom it is quite unclear whether he belonged to the family. A lawsuit in year 18 of Ramesses II was won by Khay, probably because someone had tampered with the documents. Some time afterwards, our Mose, who was Nubnofret's son, and had now come of age, reclaimed the family property before the lawcourt. Since the papers were forged, he called upon witnesses who were able to prove that he was indeed a descendant of Neshi.

Unfortunately, the end of the text with the pronouncement of the final verdict is lost, but judging by the fact that Mose inscribed the long record on the walls of his tomb we can be certain that he won the lawsuit. The case proves just how strong the force of heredity was in matters of landed property. It also shows how an estate could remain undivided for a very long period.

Such undivided properties are also encountered in one of the most important administrative documents that has come down to us from the New Kingdom. This is the Wilbour Papyrus, now in the Brooklyn Museum, New York. It is a roll over 10 metres long, bearing two texts, both of which concern fields: one of 4,500 lines in over 102 columns on the recto and part of the verso, a second of 732 lines on 25 wide pages on the remainder of the verso. The contents are very complicated, many aspects being as yet not well understood. Text A contains a tax list of numerous fields in Middle Egypt dated to year 4 of Ramesses V; Text B comprises a list of particular types of land in that area.

For our present purpose it is relevant that no less than 131 female names are recorded among the landholders. In a few cases the lady is stated as being dead; sometimes the land is said to be now in the hands of her children. This again serves to prove the continuity of family property over the generations.

Probably, the female owner inherited it from her husband or her father; in the latter case at least three generations would have owned the land. In other instances fields, some also owned by men, are said to be held "together with his/her siblings", which confirms the existence of the undivided landed properties we encountered in the story of Mose.

Such undivided plots are an indication of strong ties between the co-owners. Whether they were tilled by them as a collective we do not know. Nor is it certain that we have here an aspect of the domestic unit discussed above. Even so, it appears that, more frequently than in our society, descendants of one grandfather or great-grandfather, or even a more remote ancestor, constituted a group with a common interest. The rôle of parents and grandparents and their ties with the entire family appears to have been more important in those ancient times than in our more individualistic age. The next chapter will illustrate one special aspect of this social habit.

V The Ancestors

The Ancient Egyptians held the belief that when a person died he did not immediately vacate this world. The deceased was regarded as still being sufficiently near, particularly if he or she had been a forceful personality, to exert an influence on the affairs of the living. Such powerful dead were called *akhu*, and were distinguished from the ordinary dead.

It was a widespread custom to pour water for the deceased at his tomb. A Sixth Dynasty inscription from a Saqqara mastaba – it appears on a lintel which is now in the Cairo Museum – testifies to this practice. It is written by the tomb-owner, a certain Nedjemib, who appeals to the living with these words:

> Oh you living on earth, who will pass this tomb,
> libate for me, for I am a master of secrets;
> bring me a funerary offering from your provisions,
> for I am one who loves men.

Moving to the New Kingdom and to the famous *Instruction of Ani*, we read:

> Libate for your father and mother,
> who are resting in the desert valley.
> When the gods witness your action,
> they will say: 'Accepted'.

A similar appeal occurs in a contemporary papyrus containing a copy of the *Calendar of Lucky and Unlucky Days*. For the last day of the fourth month there is noted:

> Make an offering to the *akhu* in your house,
> make an offering to the gods.

The first clause in particular will help us to understand some of the evidence presented in this chapter.

Limestone akh iqer en Re *stela of Dhutymose (Deir el-Medina, Twentieth Dynasty). (Fig.18)*

That the instigation to libate for the dead indeed had practical results we know from certain ostraca from Deir el-Medina. In two of them it is related that the vizier came to the Theban necropolis in order to libate for the Kings of Upper and Lower Egypt, clearly the recently deceased rulers. In other texts, listing the days that particular artisans had been absent from their work in the royal tomb, there is noted as a reason for this that they had been libating for their father, or their brother, or their son. We possess no record that they did so for a woman, but that may be pure chance.

Whether this ceremony took place near the tomb or in a house (as the text quoted above stimulates the reader to do) is nowhere recorded. In one case a man even libated on three consecutive days for his father. In another ostracon we read that five men buried a certain Pay, among whom was his son; three days later three of them, including the son, plus a fourth man, went to libate. Here it is clear that the ceremony took place shortly after death, but that should not necessarily have been so in other instances.

Recently deceased members of the family were sometimes honoured by having a small stela erected to their memory. About seventy of these stelae, which are usually not more than 25 centimetres in height, are at present known from various sites in Egypt. The vast majority, however, derive from Deir el-Medina (fig. 18). They were set up in houses, invariably in a niche in the walls of the main rooms, but others have been found in the area of the temples and chapels, or even between the tombs.

On the stelae we see the dedicatee (seldom two persons) seated, or in a few cases kneeling or standing before a deity. A characteristic is that the venerated dead holds in his clenched fist the stem of a lotus flower, which curves away from his body, the flower looping back towards his nose. In all cases the main figure is designated *akh iqer en Re*, "the able spirit of Re". The word "able" implies that the person (usually a man, but there are instances in which it is a woman) was capable of acting in the Hereafter, being well-equipped with offerings and in possession of the knowledge of the correct spells to facilitate his passage through the Netherworld.

The expression *akh iqer en Re* occurs also on offering tables, on pyramidia, and on some tomb walls (see below), but the stelae are the typical products of the ancestor cult. The representation is indeed so characteristic that the question can be raised as to whether the numerous stelae with such iconographic traits all refer to the ancestor cult, although the crucial words are here absent.

An illustration of this cult is found in a scene in the mid-Nineteenth Dynasty Deir el-Medina tomb of the sculptor Nakhtamun (TT 335). A couple is depicted, seated in a kiosk, with the man holding the characteristic lotus flower. Before him stands the tomb-owner, dressed as a priest, and offering to them. They are designated in the caption as: "The servant of the Place of Truth (i.e., the necropolis workman), the lord of the house" and "His beloved wife, the mistress of the house". The spaces behind the titles, where the names should appear, have frustratingly been left blank. Clearly, however, it is ancestors who are here referred to, even though the words *akh iqer* are absent, and there is no closer indication as to exactly which forebears they are. A more specific instance is another scene in the same tomb, where the "able spirit of Re" Neferhotep receives offerings from Nakhtamun, his wife, and a long row of family members. This Neferhotep was, however, as far as we know, not an ancestor of Nakhtamun, but rather an eminent chief workman of the early Nineteenth Dynasty.

Another aspect of the ancestor cult are the so-called anthropoid busts, also called "ancestral busts" (Petrie's "oracular busts" is a misnomer). These are small human heads, resting on a support. A vague indication of the shoulders is given, but not of the chest or the arms. Their height varies from approximately 1 to 27.5 centimetres, while the material is mostly stone, although wood, clay, and faience are also attested. Some one hundred and fifty examples are known, about half of which derive from Deir el-Medina. The majority date from the New Kingdom, only a few being earlier or later.

Some heads are bald, or else they show natural hair (fig. 19a). This type is suggested to pertain to Northern Egypt. Others display a tripartite wig (fig. 19b), which is the type of the South. This wig does not imply that a woman is represented for in some cases the skin-colour is the typical dark brown tone of a man. Apart from the hair, the busts wear the broad *wesekh* collar around the support, sometimes with pendant lotus blossoms and buds at the front.

The vast majority of these objects are uninscribed, even when there is sufficient space for an inscription. Only five bear any signs: in two examples the title 'housewife' is followed by a name, and once the titles and name of the goddess Hathor appear. The latter would suggest that a deity is portrayed.

Wooden anthropoid busts: (a) with short hair (Tomb 136 at Sedment, Eighteenth Dynasty); (b) with tripartite wig (Unprovenanced, New Kingdom). (Fig. 19)

Funerary procession: four men carry a canopic shrine on a sledge (right), two men with anthropoid busts (centre), followed by a man with a mummy mask and a necklace (left) (Tomb of Haremhab (TT 78), Eighteenth Dynasty). (Fig. 20)

Generally, the heads seem to be of two different sorts. The smaller ones (those under 10 centimetres) are probably merely amulets, whereas the larger examples are actual ancestor busts, being a kind of free-standing determinative of the phrase *akh iqer*.

One ancestor bust is exceptional. Formerly part of the Gallatin private collection, it is now in the Metropolitan Museum of Art, New York, where it is still known as the Gallatin Bust. It is far larger than any other example being 41.25 centimetres in height, whereas, as stated above, the next largest busts are about 27.5 centimetres. Made of limestone, it is handsomely painted, and although its provenance is unknown, it may very well derive from Thebes or the Theban West Bank. It is such a large head that we are inclined to see it as an actual confirmation of the representation on a stela from Abydos. Here a woman called "the housewife Henut" is standing and libating before a bust placed on a high pedestal. The object in question appears to be life-size.

Equally large in proportion to the human figures are two busts carried in a funerary procession, depicted in the Eighteenth Dynasty Theban tomb (TT 78) of the military administrator Haremhab (fig. 20). Although Egyptian art is not bound to natural proportions, the relationship between the busts and their carriers, as well as to that of the

54

mummy-mask that follows them in the cortège, strongly suggests dimensions comparable to those of the Gallatin bust or even larger. However, no such heads of this type are known to us.

If our interpretation of the *akh iqer en Re* stelae and the anthropoid busts is correct, and the fact that so many had been placed in houses makes that highly likely, it means that deceased members of the family were believed to still be part of our world. Like the gods, they too could intercede on behalf of the living, in matters of daily life as well as in the Hereafter. Prayers, and especially gifts of food (funerary offerings), could influence their participation.

That deities were moved by human actions is understandable. A fine example occurs in a letter on an ostracon, sent by a carpenter of Deir el-Medina to his mother. He tells her that he swore an oath to the god to abstain from particular kinds of meat on her behalf. However, he unfortunately broke his vow and is now afraid of the consequences. Other texts confirm that the Egyptians tried to influence the gods by a promise. In the same way they tried to move the spirits of their ancestors, if they felt themselves threatened by a dead person or wronged in this life.

The *akh* one turned to was always a close relation: a parent, child, spouse, or brother, that is, someone who was still remembered, and not an ancestor of long ago. To such a person one would write a letter, either on a bowl that was placed with food in the tomb – so the dead could not miss it – or on an ostracon or a sheet of papyrus.

About a dozen of these so-called Letters to the Dead are known. Usually they are both difficult to read and to understand. This is because some were clearly written under emotional stress leading to many scribal errors. At the same time, their authors were not always highly literate. A particular problem is that the actual subject, known to the deceased, is sometimes only vaguely indicated.

One such letter is written on a bowl, now housed in the Louvre Museum. A mother writes to her son about a person who, when still alive, had threatened to bring a charge against her and her children before the divine lawcourt in the Netherworld. She beseeches her son, who has obviously also died, to denounce the accuser before the court and defend her case. Clearly, the request is preventive. The mother does not state that she has already suffered any evil. In accordance with the situation, it is not surprising that the style of the letter is calm and the hieratic hand rather clear.

Some letters stress that the deceased are dependent upon the living for their sustenance in the Hereafter. This belief is clearly expressed in a series of Coffin Texts, those spells written on Middle Kingdom coffins.

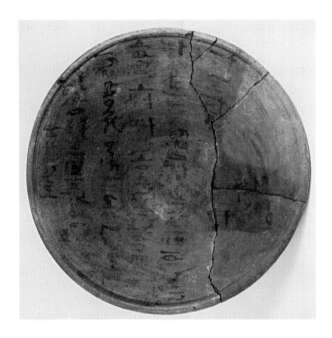

Pottery dish inscribed on the interior with a Letter to the Dead (Tomb Y84 at Hu, First Intermediate Period). (Fig. 21)

One of them, CT 38, states: "When I was in the land of the living (says a son to his deceased father), I built your altars, I established your offerings in your funerary domain". That idea we find expressed in another Letter to the Dead, the Hu Bowl (fig. 21).

Found by Petrie's assistant Arthur Mace during the 1898-99 season at the Middle Egyptian site of Hu (Diospolis Parva), this bowl is now in the Petrie Museum. It derives from Tomb Y84, which Mace's notebook reveals to be dated to the First Intermediate Period. Made of red pottery, and some 21 centimetres in diameter, it was broken into five sherds which have now been restored. The letter is addressed to "The sole friend Nefersefki" and can be translated as follows:

> The sister says to her brother:
> 'Full attention! It is profitable to pay attention to the person whom you have favoured (i.e., to me the author of the letter) on account of what is very wrongfully done to my daughter. I did nothing against him (i.e. the deceased person who threatens her). I have not consumed his property. He has not given anything to my daughter. One makes funerary offerings to a spirit (*akh*) in return for interceding on behalf of the survivor. Settle then your account with

him", who does what is painful to me, for I shall triumph against any dead man or woman who is acting against my daughter'.

This is the distressful cry of a mother to her dead brother. She has been threatened by an unnamed person that, after his death, he will bring charges against her daughter. Therefore, she begs the brother for his protection, using the argument that she has looked after him well, providing him with funerary offerings. Now it is his turn to help her.

Far clearer is a long letter, written on a sheet of fine quality papyrus, and now housed in the Leiden Museum. Its provenance is Saqqara, where it was found in the early Nineteenth Century attached to a painted wooden statuette of a woman. Also in Leiden, this, by contrast, is of inferior workmanship (fig. 22).

The Nineteenth Dynasty text is written in a nervous, rapid hand, and bristles with scribal errors, indicating that its author was in a state of high excitement. At the end the text is written in small signs and is greatly compressed as if the author noted his final sentence as an afterthought. It seems that Ankhiry's husband was rather less innocent than he pretends to be! Indeed, the entire letter makes such good reading that it deserves to be quoted extensively:

To the able spirit (*akh iqer*) Ankhiry.
'What evil thing have I done to you, that I should land in the wretched state in which I am? What have I done to you? What you have done is to lay your hands on me, although I have done you no wrong. What have I done to you since I lived with you as your husband, until that day (of your death), that I must hide it? What is there now? What you have attained is that I must bring forward this accusation against you. What have I done to you? I will lodge a complaint against you with the Ennead in the West (the divine lawcourt in the Hereafter), and one shall judge between you and me on account of this letter......

What have I done to you? I made you my wife when I was a young man. I was with you when I held all kinds of offices. I stayed with you, I did not send you away...... "She has always been with me", I thought...... And see, now you do not even comfort me. I will be judged with you, and one shall discern truth from falsehood.

Look, when I was training the officers of the army of Pharaoh and his chariotry, I let them lie on their bellies before you, and they brought all sorts of fine things to lay before you. I never hid anything from you in all your life. I never let you suffer, but I always

Painted wooden statuette of Ankhiry against the Letter to the Dead (Saqqara, Nineteenth Dynasty). (Fig. 22)

behaved to you as a gentleman. You never found that I was rude to you, as when a peasant enters someone else's house. I never behaved so that a man could rebuke me for anything I did to you......

I am sending this letter to let you know what you are doing. When you began to suffer from the disease you had, I let a head physician come and he treated you and did everything you asked him to do. When I followed Pharaoh, travelling to the south, and this condition came to you (that is, when you died), I spent no less than eight months without eating and drinking as a man should do. And as soon as I reached Memphis, I asked from Pharaoh leave and went to the place where you were, and I cried intensely, together with my people, before the eyes of my entire neighbourhood. I donated fine linen for wrapping you up, I let many clothes be made, and omitted nothing good to be done for you. And see, I passed three years until now living alone, without entering any house, although it is not fair that someone like me should be made to do so. But I did it for you, you who does not discern good from bad. One shall judge between you and me. And then: the sisters in the house, I have not entered in to anyone of them.'

The above chapter has revealed something of the rôle of the aged in Egyptian society after their death. Those who were authoritative in life were considered to exert an even more powerful influence from the next world. The beliefs of the Ancient Egyptians meant that the dead were thought to be capable of continuing to intercede, or at the worse to interfere, in the world of the living.

VI The Real and the Ideal Lifetime

In many Egyptian tombs of the New Kingdom a banquet scene is depicted at which a blind harper is represented. The song he sings is inscribed in hieroglyphs on the adjacent wall. These songs were meant to ensure blessedness for the deceased, in the meantime instructing the visitor as to the meaning and value of the mortuary cult.

Two such songs are found written before the figure of the harper (fig. 23) on a wall of the late Eighteenth Dynasty Theban tomb (TT 50) of an Amun priest (a god's father; see Chapter 8) called Neferhotep. One of these is rather exceptional. It is a glorification of death and the land of the dead, with hardly any mention of divinities or allusions to celestial topography. The following words are conspicuous:

> As to the time of activities on earth
> this is the occurrence of a dream.
> One says: 'welcome safe and sound',
> to him who reaches the West (i.e. the Netherworld).

This attitude of contempt for life on earth ("a dream") suits the context of mortuary entertainment, but in fact the opposite stance occurs even more frequently. The offering formula, in use from the Fourth Dynasty until the Ptolemaic Period, usually includes the wish for a goodly burial "after one has become very beautifully old". All sorts of additions are found at the end of the sentence, such as "in peace", "on one's seat", etc. A similar desire occurs in the conventional introduction to many a formal New Kingdom letter:

> the gods may give you Life, Prosperity, and Health,
> a long lifetime, and a great and good old age.

A long lifetime! But how old did the Ancient Egyptians actually become? Only a few cases are known. The High Priest of Amun of Karnak under Ramesses II, Bekenkhons (see p. 86) describes his career in detail on one of his statues, now in Munich (fig. 24). From this it is

Blind harper (Tomb of Neferhotep (TT 50), late Eighteenth Dynasty). (Fig. 23)

clear that he was active at least until his seventies, and probably until over eighty. In fact, if his actual words are to be trusted, we can calculate a career time-span of eighty-five years from his earliest schooldays, which means that he must have been at least ninety when he died.

An Old Kingdom nomarch from the 14th nome in Middle Egypt during the reign of Pepi II was called Pepiankh. He is also referred to as Neferka in his tomb at Meir, where the following words occur:

> I spent a lifetime until a hundred years
> among the living
> in possession of my faculties.

Whether this sentence can be accepted at face value, however, is a matter of debate.

The famous Amenhotep, son of Hapu, the favoured courtier of Pharaoh Amenhotep III, states on one of his Cairo statues:

Head of a limestone block statue of the High Priest of Amun Bekenkhons (Thebes, Nineteenth Dynasty). (Fig. 24)

> I reached eighty years, great in favour
> with the king.

To this he adds:

> I will complete 110 years.

This sentiment will be further discussed below.

Finally, there is the evidence from a Demotic Wisdom Text, known as Papyrus Insinger after the Dutch dealer who purchased it in 1895 for the Leiden Museum. The document dates from *circa* 100 A.D., and contains a description of the course of human life:

> Man spends ten years as a child before he understands
> life and death.
> He spends another ten years acquiring the work
> of instruction by which he will be able to live.

He spends another ten years gaining and earning
possessions by which to live.
He spends another ten years up to old age
before his heart takes counsel.
There remain sixty years of the whole life
which Thoth has assigned to the man of god.

The ideal lifetime is here a hundred years, but note that at forty man is
said to have reached old age!

Limestone statue of the cham-
berlain Antef. H.65 cm.
(Abydos, Twelfth Dynasty).
(Fig. 25)

Many texts refer to a good old age which was really attained, for they are found in tombs and on stelae built or erected by elderly men late in their careers. A few examples may suffice. The famous Ahmose, son of Abana, was a marine commander who accompanied Pharaoh Ahmose during his liberating campaign to expel the Hyksos from Egyptian territory (see p. 48). In the biography in his tomb at el-Kab he states:

> I have grown old,
> I have reached old age,
> Favoured as before and loved (by my Lord).
> I now [rest] in the tomb that I myself made.

Some years later, under Tuthmosis III, we have the case of Ineni, who held the post of Overseer of the Granary. He was the builder of the tomb of Tuthmosis I and of a pylon and two obelisks at Karnak. In his own Theban tomb (TT 81) he relates:

> I reached the old age of an honoured man,
> while I was daily in the favour of His Majesty
> I was fed from the table of the king
> with bread from the royal repast
> and beer likewise,
> and fat meat, various vegetables and fruits,
> honey, cakes, wine and oil.

Obviously, Ineni as a favoured servant of the king received these commodities as a sort of state pension (see Chapter 10).

These last two men and many other dignitaries relate how happy their old age was because of the favour of Pharaoh. A different boon is mentioned by the chamberlain Antef, who is known from a statue in the British Museum (fig. 25). The son of Sobkunu and Seneb, he served under Sesostris I. On one of the stelae from his offering chapel at Abydos, also in the British Museum, he says:

> I was granted to reach old age,
> with all my children holding office in the palace.

A long life was considered to be the gift of the gods. A certain Amenemope of the late Eighteenth Dynasty wrote on his cubit-rod, found at Saqqara and now in Turin (fig. 26):

> May they (the gods) give me a beautiful
> lifetime upon earth

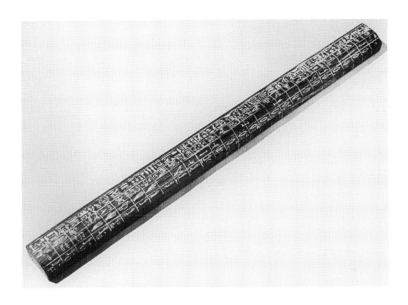

Wooden cubit-rod of Amenemope (Saqqara, late Eighteenth Dynasty). (Fig. 26)

> in the favour of the Lords Gods
> and a passing of old age without sorrows.

Even more explicit is a New Kingdom hymn to Amun, written on a papyrus housed in the Leiden Museum:

> (Amun,) who lengthens the lifetime and shortens it.
> He gives more above what is destined to him
> whom he loves.

Some Egyptians expressed a wish to pass their days in old age near the god in his temple, (probably dozing in the sun, or in the shadow of a wall, but not inside the sanctuary itself, for that was out of bounds to the laity). An example is Amenysonb from the time of Pharaoh Khendjer of the Thirteenth Dynasty. He erected a chapel at Abydos, two of the stelae of which are now in Paris and one in Liverpool. On one of the Louvre stelae (fig. 27), he says:

> The works you have done (namely, cleansing the
> Osiris temple) have now been viewed.
> As the sovereign favours you, as his *ka* favours you,
> spend your old age well in the house of your god.

Limestone stela of
Amenysonb (Abydos,
Thirteenth Dynasty).
(Fig. 27)

A similar sentiment is expressed centuries later on the stelephorous statue belonging to Nekhtefmut (see p. 46) of the Twenty-Second Dynasty. He states:

> You (Amun) have received me in my old age
> as an elderly man in your august house.

and:

You will reward me in a beautiful high age,
while I daily see Amun as I want.

Above we saw that in the late Papyrus Insinger the ideal lifetime seems to be a hundred years. In the Pharaonic Period it is frequently stated to be 110 years. Examples range from the Old Kingdom until the Late Period, but most date from the Nineteenth and Twentieth Dynasties. They occur on stelae, on statues, and on tomb walls, but also in literary texts. A variety of examples can be quoted.

In Papyrus Westcar (see p. 6) Prince Hardedef tells his father, King Snefru, about the magician Djedi:

> He is a man of 110 years,
> who eats 500 loaves of bread
> half an ox for meat,
> and drinks 100 jugs of beer, to this very day.

We have already seen that Amenhotep, son of Hapu wished in his eighties to attain 110 years. A century later, Bekenkhons, whom we calculated may have lived into his nineties, states on his Munich statue:

> May (the god) give me a beautiful lifetime
> <u>after</u> 110 years.

This is evidently spoken by Bekenkhons <u>as the statue</u> wishing to endure after death. Whatever, the sentence shows that 110 years was a standard expression.

In a New Kingdom schoolbook (see p. 99), there is a poem in which the pupil addresses wishes to his master in the form of a studied sequence of sentences. Obviously these were considered to be high art:

> May you multiply happy years,
> your months in prosperity,
> your days in life and well-being,
> your hours in health,
> your gods pleased with you;
> they being content with your utterances,
> and a goodly West having been sent forth to you.
> You are not yet old, you are not ill.
> May you complete 110 years upon earth,
> your limbs being vigorous,

as happens to one who is praised like you
when his god favours him.

Similar sentiments occur in the introduction to the *Tale of Woe*, the literary composition of Papyrus Pushkin 127 mentioned above (see p. 7):

> May he (the solar god Atum) cause you to reach
> 110 years upon earth,
> your body whole, growing old with a contented heart,
> without illness in your limbs,
> but with continuous gladness and joy in your heart,
> and without the weakness of old age,
> you having indeed arrested it.

What a beautiful wish this is!

In year 50 of Ramesses II, a scribe named Ptahemwia, travelling with his father, visited the Fifth Dynasty pyramids of Abusir. They also entered the beautiful mastaba of Ptahshepses at the site, excavated in the sixties and seventies by a Czech expedition. On one of its walls Ptahemwia, clearly an ancient vandal, recorded their visit, including the words:

> That we may reach 110 years, we pray you (the goddess).

However, the wish to live 110 years does not relate to a king. This is evident from the Great Papyrus Harris, now in the British Museum (see p. 101). It is a list of what Ramesses III had donated to the temples, drawn up by his son and successor:

> You (Amun) allotted to me a kingship of 200 years. Establish them also for my son who is (still) on earth. Make his lifetime longer than that of any other king in exchange for the benefactions I have made for your *ka*.

The ideal of 110 years also found its way into the Old Testament. In Genesis 50, verse 22, we read of Joseph:

> So Joseph dwelt in Egypt he and his father's house;
> and Joseph lived a hundred and ten years.

This is stated again in verse 26. For Joseph that is understandable as he lived in Egypt, but it is also twice stated of the successor of Moses, namely Joshua. In Joshua 24, verse 29, and Judges 2, verse 8, we read:

And Joshua the son of Nun, the servant
of the Lord, died,
being a hundred and ten years old.

It will be obvious from this chapter that, as in all societies, the actuality in terms of age attainment fell somewhat short of the desire. The real and the ideal lifetime were indeed completely different matters in Ancient Egypt.

VII The 'Staff of Old Age'

Sticks and staves were of great significance to the Egyptians. "There was scarcely any object in the life of Ancient Egypt that was so commonly in use, that was used in so many different ways, and that took so great a variety of forms". So wrote Henry Fischer, then Research Curator at the Egyptian Department in the Metropolitan Museum of Art, New York, in a 1978 review article.

Staves were a symbol of dignity for men in power. An example is that held by the Fifth Dynasty priest Ka-aper in his famous wooden statue in Cairo, commonly referred to as the Sheikh el-Beled (see p. 14), the name given to it by the Arab workmen at the time of its discovery. Women did not usually carry staves; instead they are sometimes depicted holding a stick in the shape of a long-stemmed lotus, such as that of Queen Ioh in the Wadi Shatt er-Rigal relief (see fig. 33).

Staves were also a support for the elderly, both men and women. A comparison can be drawn between the hieroglyphic sign showing a bent man leaning on a stick, which is well-distinguished from that of an upright dignitary with a stick (fig. 28a and b). In a few cases the sign portrays an old woman (fig. 28c). There are also depictions of real elderly women leaning on sticks, such as that of an old crone with dishevelled

Hieroglyphic signs: (a) for elderly and old age, clearly distinguished from (b) that for an upright dignitary; (c) picture of an old woman once used in writing the feminine word for old age (Mastaba of Ti at Saqqara, Fifth Dynasty). (Fig. 28)

Women bringing the revenue of Nubia to the Viceroy Huy. One of them, with white hair, is leaning on a stick (Tomb of Huy (TT 40), Eighteenth Dynasty). (Fig. 29)

white hair who appears as one of a group of tribute bearers in the Theban tomb of Huy (TT 40), the Viceroy of Nubia in the reign of Tutankhamun (fig. 29).

In accordance with the many tangible forms, there are also numerous words for sticks and staves. A modern study, published in 1976 by the Egyptian scholar Ali Hassan, lists seventy-four different names. However, it must be acknowledged that some are merely variants; others are very rare, perhaps mentioned only once, while yet more denote what we would call 'sceptres'. By comparison, modern Egyptian Arabic knows sixteen words for a staff or stick.

Some types are typical for a certain period. In the Old Kingdom the officials carry a long, slightly tapering staff, called a *medu* (fig. 30). By contrast, in the New Kingdom many of these artefacts have a curved projection at the top, either the natural fork of a branch, or else an imitation. Certain servants carry specific staffs. Shepherds, for example, are portrayed with a crooked or a curved staff. It is also particularly in the New Kingdom that staffs are inscribed and covered with copper and gilded tips at each end.

All sorts and types were placed in tombs, some being real objects used in life, whilst others are merely dummies made specifically for the burial equipment. Three pertinent examples of burials containing sticks

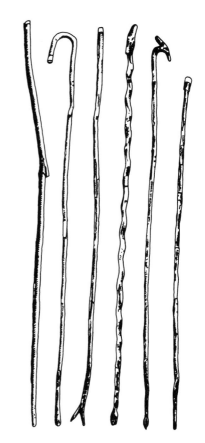

Left: Wooden figure of a standing man holding a medu-staff (Saqqara, Sixth Dynasty). (Fig. 30)

Above: Wooden staves of Senebtisi (Tomb of Senebtisi at el-Lisht, Thirteenth Dynasty). (Fig. 31)

and staves can be cited. The first are those found in the burial of a woman called Senebtisi. Her tomb at el-Lisht, situated close to the pyramid of Amenemhat I, was excavated in 1906-7 by the Metropolitan Museum of Art Expedition. A simple shaft-and-chamber tomb, it was nevertheless exceptional because of its rich contents which were practically undamaged. Despite its situation, the objects and in particular the coffins, prove that Senebtisi was buried during the Thirteenth Dynasty rather than the early Twelfth. Two sets of staves were discovered, one in a box which had suffered badly from exposure, and the other in the coffin with the body which were, by contrast, well-preserved. The latter consisted of six staves of various types, now in the Metropolitan Museum of Art (fig. 31). In itself it is surprising to find staves in a female burial, because most of them she could not have used in life. Perhaps the underlying reason was that every dead person was believed to become a (male) Osiris.

Our second instance is the intact tomb of Kha, the architect of Amenhotep III, discovered at Deir el-Medina in 1906 by the Italian archaeologist Ernesto Schiaparelli. Kha possessed ten sticks and staves of varying diameters, four being very thin and the remainder solid. Two of the latter are decorated with bronze inlays and incised with the name and title of their owner. In addition to *medu*-staves, there are six forked examples; in three cases the protruding element had been artificially fixed, whilst in the others it was natural. Two of Kha's walking sticks had been broken and repaired in antiquity by winding papyrus bark around the breakage. Obviously they were both precious and well-used!

Thirdly, we have the burial of Tutankhamun with its amazing total of 130 sticks and staves, seventy of these being of the *medu*-type. A large bundle of them was found, leaning against the wall, between the first and second catafalques. Some were ornamented with bark, while others were gilded or even embellished with gold. Special attention should be paid to four ceremonial staves which are real works of art, their lower ends being decorated with beautifully carved figures of Nubians, and, in one case, a Nubian and a Syrian back to back. In stuccoed, gilded, and painted wood, the face and arms of the Nubians are made of ebony, those of the bearded Syrian of ivory. Sadly, all Tutankhamun's sticks and staves still await definitive publication.

Their fundamental rôle in daily life led to a particular metaphoric use of the staff, especially of the *medu*. On a Fifth Dynasty stela in Cairo, the owner, a certain Hemmin, calls himself a "pillar of old age". A similar expression occurs on the Twelfth Dynasty stela of Nesmontu, now in Paris. In his laudatory autobiography the owner states of himself:

> I was a support of the aged,
> a nurse of the little ones.

Yet another phrase, encountered in the Old Kingdom, is "staff of old people". This concept developed into a fixed expression: "staff of old age", in which "staff" is written with the word for *medu*. As we shall see, the idiom carried a specific meaning.

The oldest known instance of its use is found in the *Instruction of Ptahhotep*. As stated above (see p. 5), Ptahhotep was a Fifth Dynasty vizier, but the earliest text of his *Instruction*, which is now in the Bibliothèque Nationale in Paris, dates in fact from the Middle Kingdom (see p. 83). It is in this text that the phrase "staff of old age" occurs. Therefore, it has been suggested that this is a later addition. After setting forth the evils of old age (see p. 5), Ptahhotep asks the king:

> May this servant be ordered to make
> a 'staff of old age',
> and let his son step in his place,
> so as to tell him the words of those who heard,
> the ways of the ancestors
> who have listened to the gods.

A second instance from the Middle Kingdom occurs in the tomb of the nomarch Dhutihotep II at el-Bersheh, who was a contemporary of Sesostris II and III. Dhutihotep's father Kay is portrayed standing face to face with him and stating, according to the text above the figures, that "my lord" and "my god" (i.e., the king):

> made my son to be chief of his city
> and overlord of the Hare (the 15th) nome
> in the place of him who created me.

In other words, Dhutihotep must have directly succeeded Nehri, Kay's father and his grandfather. Could this perhaps have been because Kay was too old to shoulder the duties of a nomarch? The son then says of his father:

> He made me to be chief of his city
> and overlord of the Hare nome
> in the place of him who begot him.
> He (Kay) was the 'staff of old age'
> of his father (Nehri),
> he made me to be chief of his city.

The figures of father and son both hold *medu*-staffs in their hands. This face to face depiction is the antithesis of the usual Old Kingdom scene where the tomb-owner, either sitting or standing, is portrayed with a diminutive figure of a son clinging to his father's staff (fig. 32). Such a gesture of dependence is here transposed into one of equality.

The phrase "staff of old age" also occurs in administrative texts. In a Kahun papyrus (see p. 37), a father, an overseer of priests, certifies that he hands over his office to his son:

74

Representation of Hetepherakhet on the right side of the entrance to his mastaba-chapel. His eldest son, pictured as a boy, is clinging to his staff (Saqqara, Fifth Dynasty). (Fig. 32)

to be a 'staff of old age', for I am old.
Let Pharaoh appoint him immediately.

There are also three instances of the phrase known from the New Kingdom. One features in a narrative concerning the installation of the vizier User(amun) as the successor of his father Iahmose (see p. 45). It is written on a wall in one of the son's Theban tombs (TT 131).

It relates how, during a throne-session King Tuthmosis II makes an allusion to the age of his vizier. The courtiers, standing around the throne, answer him:

You have perceived, O Sovereign, our lord,
that the vizier has reached old age.
Some bowing down came to his back ......

It may be useful to your two lands
to look out for a 'staff of old age'.

Then Pharaoh orders the search for a suitable candidate, and the
courtiers, after having considered several possibilities, suggest the vizier's
son User(amun), for:

Intelligent and of good character,
he is suitable for a 'staff of old age'.

The king agrees with them and confirms:

I have recognized your (Iahmose's) son User(amun)
as efficacious and persevering and righteous
[through] your instruction ......
May his virtues serve you,
so that he be to you a 'staff of old age'.

This is a composition of the "Königsnovelle" type, the name given
by Egyptologists to a particular literary genre in which an important
historical decision by the Pharaoh is related. For instance, the building of
a temple, the dispatching of an expedition, or the commencement of a
war. The usual setting is a session of the king's council, either political or
military, during which the king makes a speech. His advisors reply with
cautious considerations or objections, and then the king takes a bold
decision – which of course turns out to be the right one.

The second New Kingdom example of the idiom occurs in the
autobiography of the High Priest of Amun Amenemhat, from the reign
of Amenhotep II. Cast in the form of a wisdom text, it is inscribed on a
wall in the inner room of his Theban tomb (TT 97). He tells his children:

I was a priest, and a 'staff of old age' with my father
while he was living on earth.

This father, called Dhutihotep, was a simple lay priest, overseer of sandal
makers in the Temple of Karnak. So it appears that even humble temple
servants had a 'staff of old age'.

That not only high officials received such a helpmate, is also clear
from our third instance, a sentence in the autobiography of Amenhotep,
son of Hapu (see p. 61), written on his limestone block statue in Cairo.
Describing his early career as a military administrator, he states:

I recruited the young men of my lord,
my reed pen counted their numbers by millions.
I made them into companies
in the place of the members of their families
a 'staff of old age' as his beloved son.

In conclusion it can be stated that "staff of old age" is a figurative expression to describe a son who was appointed, by the Pharaoh or by a bureaucrat, to act as the deputy and future successor of his father, while the latter still officially retained his authority. It seems to have been a special administrative title and as such is attested only from the Middle Kingdom and the Eighteenth Dynasty. The phrase itself reflects the prominent rôle of staves in the life of Ancient Egypt.

VIII The 'God's Father'

One of the most curious titles from Ancient Egypt is that of the 'god's father'. An exact rendition of the Egyptian phrase *it-netjer* is 'father of the god'. Earlier Egyptologists habitually translated the expression as 'divine father', but that is not correct. Regrettably, this error is sometimes still perpetuated today. The god here is actually the king, although, as we shall see, it is very seldom the preceding Pharaoh who is so designated.

The origin of the epithet is unknown: perhaps it started out as a court title, later, by the time of the Old Kingdom, becoming an honorary one. Indeed, a peculiar characteristic is that although the term remained in vogue throughout Egyptian history, it changed its meaning several times. The connecting element was that it designated a high rank thus defining the relationship of the bearer with the king. That may be a family tie, or also the ideal fathership as the tutor of the future Pharaoh, but should not necessarily be so. A chronological survey citing specific instances will serve to illustrate this point.

The Sixth Dynasty Pharaoh Pepi I married the two daughters of a local ruler at Abydos named Khuy. At the same point their brother Djau became the vizier. The girls both received the new name of Ankhes-en-Meryre (literally "She-lives-for-Meryre", Meryre being the *prenomen* of Pepi I). They subsequently became the mothers of the successive Pharaohs Merenre and Pepi II, the latter of whom is credited with a ninety year reign (see p. 114). On account of his strong ties to the monarch, Khuy was called "god's father, god's beloved". Here in fact the title can simply be interpreted as father-in-law of the king.

Several other persons from the late Old Kingdom and the succeeding periods are called "god's father", but for what reason we do not know. That they were all related to the Pharaoh is unlikely. That is only the case with some of them. During the First Intermediate Period the Vizier Shemay erected a series of stelae in the Temple of Min at Coptos, all of which are inscribed with royal decrees. From these it appears that Shemay was married to a royal princess called Nebet, and perhaps for that reason he bore the title "god's father, god's beloved". The same designation is also given to the son of Shemay and Nebet. But in this case they were not fathers-in-law, but rather a son-in-law and grandson of the reigning king!

Later in the First Intermediate Period and during the early Eleventh Dynasty the title underwent a distinct change in meaning. In the temple of the deified Heqaib (the surname of an Old Kingdom governor and caravan leader Pepinakht) on the island of Elephantine at Aswan, three fragmentary quartzite statues were found during the excavations of the great Egyptian archaeologist Labib Habachi. The statues are now housed in the Aswan Museum on the island. One is totally uninscribed, another bears the name of Wahankh Antef, an early ruler of the Eleventh Dynasty, while the third carries the inscription "gods' father (note the plural here) Montuhotep-aa", the name being in a cartouche. All three statues are clearly in the same style and were probably made by the same sculptor. Although Montuhotep-aa was certainly not a Pharaoh, this statue portrays him as a man dressed as a king in the royal kilt and seated upon a throne. The explanation seems to be that he was the father of two rulers, namely Sehertawy Antef (I) and Wahankh Antef (II). Therefore *it-netjer* here indeed designates the (non-royal) father of a king.

The same meaning is encountered in an Eighteenth Dynasty inscription on a block from a building of Amenhotep I at Karnak. This

Rock relief of Montuhotep II and his mother Ioh faced by the "god's father" King Antef and the chancellor Khety (Wadi Shatt er-Rigal, Eleventh Dynasty). (Fig. 33)

Diorite statue of Senenmut
carrying the Princess
Neferure (Karnak,
Eighteenth Dynasty).
(Fig.34)

lists the names of earlier Pharaohs, still revered in later ages. Those of the Eleventh Dynasty rulers Nebhepetre (Montuhotep II) and Seankhkare (Montuhotep III) are followed by that of "the god's father Sesostris". He can be identified as the non-royal father of Amenemhat I, the founder of the Twelfth Dynasty.

Montuhotep II is also depicted on a spectacular rock relief in the Wadi Shatt er-Rigal, situated some four kilometres north of Gebel Silsileh on the west bank of the Nile (fig. 33). It was here that the sandstone was quarried for the king's innovative mortuary temple at Deir el-Bahri. The large incised relief, which measures some 2 metres high by 2.15 metres wide, portrays a practically life-sized King Nebhepetre Montuhotep, followed by his mother Ioh, with before him "the god's father, god's beloved, the son of Re Antef". The name is written in a cartouche, and the figure is clearly dressed as a king with the royal kilt and bull's tail, the *nemes* headdress, and the royal uraeus on his brow. The chancellor Khety follows directly behind him, his right hand upon his breast in a respectful position of salute. Who this Antef was is not clear, but it is conceivable that we can identify him as Montuhotep's bodily father. This Antef had indeed been kinglet at Thebes, but he was never King of Upper and Lower Egypt. Therefore he was theoretically not the predecessor (= the "father") of Montuhotep. What is announced in this scene is probably the divine marriage of Ioh that led to the birth of a new (the Eleventh) Dynasty.

The early Thirteenth Dynasty, which is now called the late Middle Kingdom, has as its two most prominent rulers the brothers Khasekhemre Neferhotep (I) and Khaneferre Sebekhotep (IV). They were the sons of a commoner named Haankhef. The father is designated on their monuments and scarabs as *it-netjer*. Here again the title seems to point to the (non-royal) father of the ruling Pharaoh, but so far as we know this is the last instance in Egyptian history.

The Eighteenth Dynasty witnesses a fundamental change in the meaning of the title, many important persons now being called *it-netjer*, with the implication of advisor of the sovereign or elder statesman. Some examples are: various High Priests of Amun, such as Amenemhat (see p. 76), who enjoyed an unusual late career under Amenhotep II; viziers, such as Rekhmire under Tuthmosis III; and Viceroys of Nubia, such as Usersatet, a childhood companion of Amenhotep II.

A suggestion has been made that the designation now means tutor of the crown-prince (or princess). A fine example would be that of Senenmut, the favourite and *éminence grise* of Queen Hatshepsut, who lists among his many titles that of "steward of the estate of Princess Neferure", the young daughter of the monarch. On earlier statues he calls himself "father and (male) nurse" of the princess; on one of them the text reads:

> I brought up the eldest daughter of the King,
> the god's wife Neferure, may she live,
> and I was given to her as 'father of the goddess',
> because I was so useful to the King.

Note that Hatshepsut is here referred to by the masculine designation "King", whereas Neferure bears the feminine epithet "goddess".

Probably the statue on which these words were inscribed dates from a later stage in Senenmut's career, when his pupil needed not so much a "nurse" as a mentor. The statue in question is now in the Chicago Field Museum of Natural History (fig. 34). Made of diorite and some 53 centimetres high, the standing Senenmut here carries the princess on his arms.

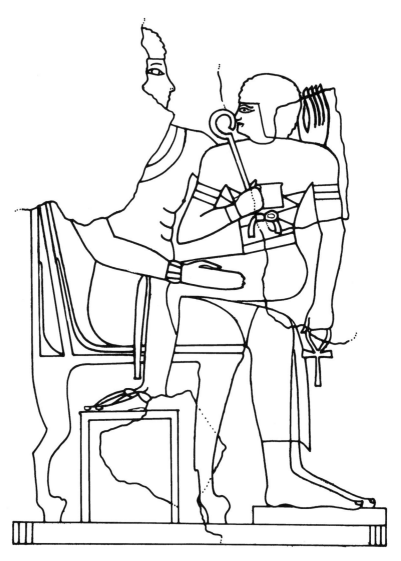

Heqareshu with Tuthmosis IV in full regalia on his lap (Theban tomb 226, Eighteenth Dynasty). (Fig. 35)

Although numerous of his statues show him with badly damaged features, this is one of the five known examples to have survived entirely intact.

The dignitary Heqareshu, who lived slightly later in the Eighteenth Dynasty, is depicted in the Theban tomb ascribed to him (TT 226) in a unique wall-painting with four princes – all with sidelocks – on his knee. In his son's tomb (TT 64) there is another representation of him with Tuthmosis IV in full regalia, on his lap (fig. 35). His titles above include those of "(male) nurse of the king's eldest son Tuthmosis (IV)" and "god's father". In front of him stands his son Heqaerneheh, the owner of the vault, with one prince before him and six others, now largely destroyed, following him. Father and son were doubtless the tutors of young royals - the father of the future Tuthmosis IV and the son of at least three, and possibly even seven, royal princes. However, it is not certain whether it was indeed the educational aspect that was here expressed by the term "god's father". The son never bears the title which could perhaps be explained by the fact that when this scene was painted Heqaerneheh's pupil Amenhotep, if he indeed was the future Pharaoh Amenhotep III, had not yet become king. However, in general doubts can be raised whether *it-netjer* ever means more than spiritual 'father' of the sovereign, that is, elder statesman.

From earlier times there is only one, highly dubious, instance of *it-netjer* as a title of a tutor of a crown-prince. The epithet is borne by the Fifth Dynasty vizier Ptahhotep (see pp. 5 and 74), at least in the manuscript of his famous *Instruction* known as Papyrus Prisse, which is now in the Bibliothèque Nationale in Paris. This version is the most complete, differing considerably from the other three known copies. The designation occurs in the introduction to the actual maxims where, between other titulary, Ptahhotep calls himself:

god's father, god's beloved, eldest son of the king, of his body, governor of the city and vizier.

The combination of "father" of Pharaoh as well as "eldest son" seems very strange until we remember that the latter is purely honorific. Whether the first epithet indeed means that he was responsible for the education of a later Pharaoh is quite uncertain, especially as it is equally unsure whether Ptahhotep himself was really so called. At least we know of no relationship of this vizier to a crown-prince. Could it already in this case be an honorary title equivalent to elder statesman such as it was later to become?

Confirmation of such an honorary title is found in Genesis 45, verse 8, where Joseph says of himself that God made him to be "a father of Pharaoh". This would seem to be a correct translation of *it-netjer*, as it clearly has the meaning here of advisor or elder statesman.

It may be that the many high dignitaries occasionally called 'god's father' played a (minor) rôle in the education of princes. An example is

Aper-el, the "forgotten vizier" of Amenhotep III, whose tomb was rediscovered in 1976 by a French expedition working at Saqqara. He was certainly not the king's father-in-law, but seems to have been a tutor of his son Amenhotep (the future Akhenaten). At least he is once called in his tomb "nurse of the royal children".

Ay shows off his new red gloves, a reward from Akhenaten and Nefertiti (Tomb of Ay at el-Amarna, Eighteenth Dynasty). (Fig. 36)

There is a possibility that some high priests initiated their royal pupils into the secrets of temple ritual, and likewise that high officials may have imparted the code of politics. A modern example of the latter practice is that of the *Raadpensionaris* (Grand Pensionary, that is Secretary of State) of Holland Jan de Witt, who acted as one of the tutors of the Prince of Orange. The young man in question was later to become *Stadhouder* in the Netherlands and King William III of England.

The most famous 'god's father' is Ay, the high official who eventually became Pharaoh at the end of the Eighteenth Dynasty. Before him the title was borne by Yuya, the father of Queen Teye, the "Great Consort" of Amenhotep III, and the mother of Akhenaten. Hence Yuya was really the father-in-law of the reigning Pharaoh. Whether this was the reason for his title, or whether it was granted to him because he was a special advisor of the monarch remains uncertain. Anyhow, he and his wife Thuyu were even afforded a burial in the Valley of the Kings (KV 46).

Ay was married to another Teye, the wet-nurse of Nefertiti. That he was also the tutor of Akhenaten and later of Tutankhamun is not quite certain. But his relations to the royal family were particularly close. Again, we are uncertain whether he owed the title 'god's father' to a post as tutor of two kings, or to his prominent position at the court of el-Amarna.

The famous recompense scene in Ay's private tomb, situated to the east of the city, depicts his official investiture by Akhenaten and Nefertiti. In one particular vignette we see him, weighed down by gold collars, proudly showing off his brand new red leather gloves (fig. 36). Gloves were extremely rare imports in Ancient Egypt: they are seldom depicted on New Kingdom reliefs, another instance being those worn by the military general Horemhab in his Saqqara tomb, and are known only from tangible linen examples found in Tutankhamun's burial. Their presentation to Ay is therefore a clear indication of the high esteem in which this bureaucrat was held. Indeed, it is even possible that we can identify Ay as the spiritual father of the whole Amarna movement.

When he became Pharaoh after the untimely death of Tutankhamun, the by now elderly statesman took the epithet *it-netjer* into his cartouche as part of his private name (*nomen*). Probably he felt that this stressed his link to the dynasty and constituted his only legitimation. However, Ay's emphasis on the title may very well equally be what brought it into discredit for statesmen, for in this position it now disappeared.

However, one notable use of *it-netjer* does occur in the Nineteenth Dynasty when Ramesses II calls his father Seti I his "god's father, god's beloved". Here, exceptionally, the title is used for a royal father!

This apart, there was from the Middle Kingdom onwards a totally different meaning, namely, that indicating a lower priestly rank.

Henceforth, it remained the only use of the title. Its relative status clearly emerges in the famous Late Twentieth Dynasty *Onomasticon of Amenope* (see p. 7) in the section listing all categories of priests and temple employees, starting with the highest grades and descending to menial occupations such as butchers and milkmen. The series begins with prophets (literally "god's servants"), the highest ranking priests, followed by *it-netjer* and then *wab* (literally "pures"), the ordinary priests. From this it appears evident that 'god's father' occupied a transitional position in the hierarchy.

An apt illustration is found in the long career of Bekhenkhons (see fig. 24 and pp. 60 and 67), the High Priest of Amun at Karnak under Ramesses II. After a primary school education and a training job he passed four years as a *wab* priest. Perhaps this was simply a part-time post during his training as an administrator. Then he started to climb the hierarchical ladder as an *it-netjer*, at which level he stayed for twelve years. Afterwards he became successively Third Prophet of Amun, Second Prophet, and finally High Priest. It is clear that 'god's father' marks the transition to the higher echelons of the priesthood.

One of Bekhenkhons' successors was a man called Rome-Roy, who was active under Merneptah and his descendants. He describes his career on one of his statues now in Cairo. As a *wab* priest he was chosen, he states, because of his eminent qualities to be introduced to the function of *it-netjer* in order to serve the *ka* of the god.

This is an indication of what we now have to understand by the title. At a certain moment in their life, some of the *wab* priests were inducted as *it-netjer* to serve the cult images of the deity, hidden away in the innermost sanctuaries, where ordinary priests were not allowed to enter. These *wab* priests could indeed serve the processional statues, but remained excluded from real responsibilities and, unlike the *it-netjer*, were not initiated into the secrets of the cult.

It will be evident that 'god's father' could refer to several quite different positions and functions during the long period of Egyptian history. Yet, the word 'father' retained throughout the notion of veneration, whether it referred to a real father (-in-law) of the reigning king, to a wise advisor of the sovereign, or merely to a priest who was initiated into the secrets of the god.

IX Care of the Elderly

In Chapter 4 we argued that the position of the elderly in a particular society depends to a large extent on their ties with their descendants. Older people without offspring are therefore rather helpless. They are forced to rely on the care and assistance of neighbours and distant relatives, generally less reliable than one's own children. Hence, if one wishes to avoid the situation that one will eventually be alone, it is necessary to generate offspring. Children are the insurance against the deprivations of old age. But what if one is not lucky in this matter? There are in general three possible strategies for the childless: adoption, divorce and remarriage, and polygamy.

Adoption certainly occurred in Ancient Egypt, but we have no idea how frequently. This is not helped by the fact that it is sometimes difficult to distinguish true adoption from the practice of taking a foster-child. In this connection a letter on a Deir el-Medina ostracon is of relevance. Dating to the Ramesside Period, it is now in Berlin. The unnamed sender states:

> He who has no children should get for himself some orphan to bring him up. Then he will be the person who pours water upon his hands, as a genuine eldest son.

Whether this refers to a formal legal adoption is very much an open question. But it certainly reveals a means of acquiring essential care in old age.

In general not much is known about adoption. A special case was that of the Divine Adoratrices, particularly during the Third Intermediate Period. These women were envisaged as being the consorts of the god Amun; they were therefore nominally, perhaps in many cases also actually, head of the Karnak Temple with its extensive properties and large personnel. Since they had to be virgins, they adopted their successors, who were the sisters or daughters of the rulers. This proves that formal adoption was not unknown.

One papyrus, dating from the late New Kingdom, provides us with information concerning the legal formalities. Originally in the possession of Sir Alan Gardiner, he donated it in 1945 to the Ashmolean Museum, Oxford. The text, deriving from Middle Egypt, is known as "The Adoption Papyrus" and consists of two parts.

The first lines relate how in year 1 of Ramesses XI, on the exact day of his accession, a certain Nebnofre adopted his wife as his own daughter. The reason was that their marriage had remained childless. In this way Nebnofre could leave all his properties to his wife after his death, and claims of his siblings would be invalid. The adoption took place before witnesses, while the sister of Nebnofre was also present.

Seventeen years later the present document was drawn up by the wife. She relates in the introduction what we have summarized above. She continues by telling that Nebnofre, together with her, had purchased a female slave, who had subsequently given birth to two girls and a boy. Doubtless, Nebnofre was their father. The wife took care of the children, probably because Nebnofre had by then died, and they in turn behaved well towards her. She had then married the eldest girl to her younger brother Padiu, at the same time emancipating her. Now she adopts her brother, emancipates the other two slave-children and adopts them too, declaring that all four should inherit equally from her, while Padiu will act as the trustee. He has, in exchange, to look after her in her situation as an elderly widow.

There has been much discussion concerning the correct interpretation of this text, for the scribe was incredibly incompetent. Gardiner called the language "barbarous" and the composition of the document "execrable". Although in most of the text the words are those of the woman, he almost always uses the masculine pronoun, so that it has been suggested that it was Nebnofre who adopted the children. We believe, however, following Gardiner, that the above is a correct reconstruction of the events. Evidently, adoption was a means to provide for a childless woman after she became a widow.

Another method to try and acquire offspring in old age would be to divorce a childless wife and to marry another woman. Divorce in itself was easy. Since there seems to have been no ceremonial wedding, it was possible to dissolve the tie with hardly any formality. In the Leiden Letter to the Dead quoted above (see pp. 57-59), the husband stresses that he did not send away his wife whom he had married as a youth. That was clearly not self-evident. Note that, so far as we know, the marriage had remained childless. At least, no offspring are mentioned.

Divorce seems to have been particularly common among the mass of the population during the Ramesside Period. This is revealed by the

Tomb Robbery Papyri, an archive from the later reigns of the Twentieth Dynasty dealing with the investigations and trials of the people who had plundered several private and some royal tombs. Among the culprits were many labourers and lower grade priests, but also a few more influential persons. We find some indications of what may be divorce in these papyri. Once a woman even testifies before the Court:

> I am one of four wives (of a goldsmith Ramose), two being dead and another still alive.

It is of course not certain whether Ramose had divorced the latter, and whether such separations without a formal wedding could be called 'divorce' is a matter of terminology. Moreover, it is nowhere stated that such 'divorces' took place because of the woman's inability to bear children. Yet, that certainly seems a possibility.

None the less, 'divorces' for such a reason were clearly not the general practice. From Deir el-Medina, the Village which has yielded so much relevant information on real life, we know of at least two important men who never had their own offspring. One is the scribe (administrator) Ramose, from the reign of Ramesses II. He was obviously a notable and a rich man, for he built no less than three tombs for himself and erected many stelae and statues. Although he could easily have afforded a second wife, he adopted a young scribe called Qenhikhopshef, who acted as his son and successor.

Another example is the chief workman Neferhotep, whose marriage with Ubekht also remained sterile. The couple first adopted a certain Paneb, the son of one of the workmen, but he grew up to be a

Relief of Hesysunebef with a pet monkey, on the side of a fragmentary seated statue of Neferhotep and his wife Ubekht (Tomb of Neferhotep (TT 216), Nineteenth Dynasty). (Fig. 37)

Mery-aa and his wives: (above) Mery-aa himself with his ?first wife Isi; (below) his five other wives (Tomb of Mery-aa at el-Hagarseh, Ninth Dynasty). (Fig. 38)

particularly nasty intriguer and bully. Later on they chose as *protégé* a slave-boy called Hesysunebef ("His lord may praise him") (fig. 37). That proved much more successful. This man remained loyal to his former master and mistress, and when he was later set free and married he called his son after the former and his daughter after the latter. What is relevant here is that the marriage of these two seems to have remained stable despite their childlessness.

It is mostly difficult to ascertain whether in a particular case we have to do with divorce when a tomb-owner appears to have had more than one wife. For instance, in the Nineteenth Dynasty tomb of the High Priest of Onuris Anhermose (see fig. 42) at el-Mashayikh (situated not far from Abydos, near the modern town of Girga, in Middle Egypt), two successive wives are recorded. One of them is called on a statue: "his former wife". Does that mean that he had divorced her, or did she die before he remarried? Perhaps the latter, for we would not expect her to appear on the tomb walls if the marriage had broken down.

Somewhat clearer is the situation alluded to in an ostracon from Deir el-Medina. There a man lists the objects which remained in his house: "after he left Wabe, his first wife". He seems to have moved into a new partnership, while being unable to take with him his valuables, for the list enumerates a fair number of bronze objects, mainly vessels but also a razor, and their total worth is not insignificant. It is, however, far from certain that the man had left his wife because she remained childless.

Generally, the Egyptians were monogamous, only the king being accustomed to have a plurality of wives. On the other hand, there is no indication that polygamy was forbidden. Certainly not by law, but it seems not to have been frowned upon. Nowhere in the wisdom texts do the authors utter objections, although they stress the value of marrying. There exist a few indications that among the upper classes polygamy did occur, and it may well be that the wish for male offspring was behind this practice.

The strongest argument for the occurrence of polygamy is the depiction in a tomb of two wives, as in the case of Anhermose, although, as we have seen, that in itself is no proof. Perhaps more convincing is the case of Mery-aa from el-Hagarseh (near Sohag) in whose Ninth Dynasty tomb no less than six women are portrayed, all called "his wife" (fig. 38). Five of them appear to have had children. That he divorced all five is highly unlikely; he certainly would not then have had them depicted in his tomb. The childless wife Isi seems to be the most important, featuring on several walls. Was she perhaps the first, and did she remain barren?

In this case a multiple marriage seems certain. In all others it is no more than a possibility. Whatever, it was certainly rare, but its public acknowledgement in a tomb like this suggests that it was socially acceptable. Another example may be that of Khnumhotep II, the son of Nehri (see p. 46). In his tomb at Beni Hasan two wives are mentioned, but, as with Anhermose, it may be that the first had died before he married the heiress of the 17th nome.

Once again, it is one of the Tomb Robbery Papyri that provides us with a rather clear instance. In a list of women involved in the affair, one of them, who is named Herer, is said to be the wife of a guard of Pharaoh's Treasury. The next one, in the following line, is called "his other wife, which makes two". This strongly suggests that the guard was living with both women at the same time.

It is time to return to our main subject, namely, the care of the elderly. It was particularly the position of single women that caused difficulties. Therefore, the wisdom texts devote some attention to widows. So, for example, the *Instruction* addressed to King Merikare, which dates from the First Intermediate Period, the author says to his son, the future Pharaoh:

> Do justice, then you endure on earth;
> Calm the weeper, don't oppress the widow,
> Don't expel a man from his father's property.

Then there are the words of the New Kingdom *Instruction of Amenemope*:

> Do not encroach on the boundaries of a widow,

and elsewhere:

> Do not pounce on a widow when you find her
> in the fields.

That means, when she is gleaning on your land. This situation reminds us of the famous Old Testament picture of Ruth and Boaz.

In all these cases it is not stated that the widow is old. Even young widows without the protection of a husband were considered to be vulnerable, but that held especially true for those who were elderly.

The famous vizier Rekhmire states in his autobiography in his Theban tomb (TT 100) among a catalogue of his good deeds:

> I have protected the widow who had no husband.

Further on, he says:

> I provided for the old one while I gave [him my staff],
> causing the old women to say: 'That is good'.

One of the most stringent duties of every high official towards the aged was to bury the dead. To declare that this had been carried out belongs to the traditional subjects of a Middle Kingdom autobiography. For example, the priest Wepwawet-aa, from the time of Sesostris I and Amenemhat II, writes on his stela, erected at Abydos and now in Leiden:

> I buried the old ones in my town.

In many instances this common sentence in the 'moral profile' is followed by its counterpart:

> I brought up the children.

Care for both vulnerable categories, the elderly and the younger generation, is thus juxtaposed.

Another aspect of the relationship between the generations is found on the Twelfth Dynasty stela of the police officer Beb, also in Leiden. He says:

> I handed over my office to my son
> while I was still alive.
> I made for him a testament
> in excess of what my father had made [for me],
> my house being established on its foundation,
> my fields being in their place.

That this was appreciated by the son appears evident from the following line:

> It is my son who made my name live upon this stela.

Note that the stela was erected by the son, despite the words; he thus demonstrates that he has fulfilled his filial duties.

In one case such behaviour even extended to the preceding generation. On a statue from the Late Period, now in Rome, which belongs to a certain Hor-Re and was erected by his grandson Teos, the grandfather speaks:

> He (the grandson) erected the statue beside Hathor,
> the Mistress (that is, in her temple),
> after he had interred me in a beautiful burial.
> He renewed the burial, with ointment and linen
> from the temple, after thirty-three years.

Evidently, long after his death the young man still showed his care for and devotion to his grandfather.

A unique illustration of the love of a son for his father is found in the tomb of Djau at Deir el-Gebrawi, from the time of Pepi II. Djau was a nomarch of the 12th Upper Egyptian nome and the successor of his father, who was also called Djau with the "beautiful name" Shemay. On the walls of his tomb father and son are once depicted of equal height and standing face to face, the father with a *medu*-staff in his hand (fig. 39). In a text elsewhere in the tomb the son says:

> I made that I was buried in one tomb
> with this Djau (the father),
> in order to be with him in one place,
> not because I did not have
> the means to make two tombs.
> I did it in order to see this Djau daily,
> in order to be with him in one place.

All the preceding, and even this last instance, remain on a high, rather idealized level. But what about the everyday reality? Unfortunately, the evidence is not abundant. One example is a stela found in the temple of Amen-Re at Amara-West, which is some distance South of the Second Cataract, deep into Nubia. Dating from the late Ramesside Period, a second prophet of that temple called Hori, who erected the stela, relates two different dispositions. Firstly, he declares that all the properties of his father, consisting of fields, meadows, slaves, etc., will go to his sister Irytekh. Secondly, the mother of Hori states about all the goods left to her by her husband (Hori's father) that:

> they may be given to my daughter, for she has
> acted for me when I was old.

Did, perhaps, Hori not want to care for his ageing mother, and had he for this reason promised his properties to his sister Irytekh, who had looked after the old lady and, therefore, inherited from her?

As always, the ostraca from Deir el-Medina present a picture of the reality. In one of them, now in Glasgow, and probably dating from the reign of Ramesses IV, the necropolis workman Usekhnemte ("Wide of Strides") declares that he has given all kinds of goods to his father. Some of them were luxuries: cakes, meat, fat and honey, to which he added clothes; others were basic food, bread and beer. In particular he gave him $2\frac{1}{2}$ sacks of emmer-wheat monthly, over a ten month period. As is so many times the case, the figures are somewhat mysterious, for Usekhnemte says that the total amounted to $27\frac{1}{2}$ sacks. That is either eleven times $2\frac{1}{2}$, or ten times $2\frac{3}{4}$ sacks!

The editor of the text suggests that the son here serves as the 'staff of old age' of his father. Whether he would ever have called it so is

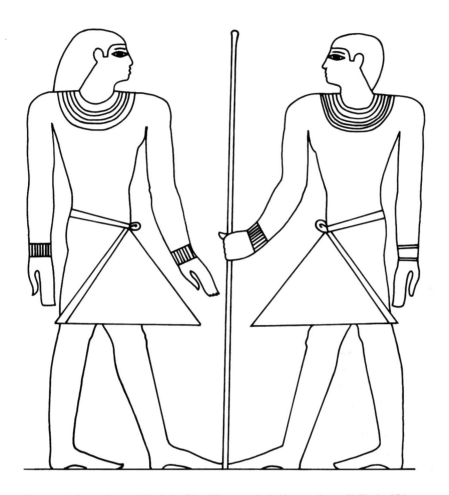

Djau stands face to face with his father Djau/Shemay, who holds a medu-*staff (Tomb of Djau at Deir el-Gebrawi, Sixth Dynasty). (Fig. 39)*

doubtful, but clearly he was not mean. His own monthly ration consisted of 4 sacks of emmer (*circa* 300 litres), of which more than half was handed over to his father. This would have been more than sufficient for the old man's personal needs, leaving even room for some dependant or servant.

Another case is mentioned in an ostracon now in the Petrie Museum (fig. 40). It is dated to the second year of Sethnakht, the first ruler of the Twentieth Dynasty. In the first lines we are told that, when Hesysunebef (see p. 90) divorced his wife, the author, whose name nowhere occurs, gave her every single month over a three year period 1

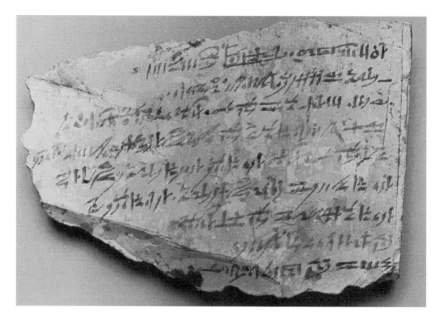

Limestone ostracon relating the charity shown by a man to a divorced woman (Deir el-Medina, Twentieth Dynasty). (Fig. 40)

oipe (*circa* 20 litres) of emmer-wheat, in total 9 sacks. He also records that he paid her for a shawl which was so worn out that it was refused on the market. Why this was written down, even to the extent of recording the names of some people who handed over his grain to the woman, that is, who were witnesses to his charity, we do not know. Had the woman perhaps died, and did the author of the ostracon claim the inheritance?

Not all children were generous towards the older generation. In a famous papyrus, now in Oxford, a lady called Naunakhte formulated her last will. Before a large section of members of the community, she declares that she has brought up her nine children and given them all that was appropriate for those in their station. Now, however, that she has grown old, not all of them have looked after her. Therefore, she disinherits one son and three daughters. Of one daughter who will still inherit she specifies:

> She shall have her share in the division of all my property, except for the *oipe* of emmer-wheat, which my three male children and one daughter have given to me, and except for my one *hin* (*circa* ½ litre) of fat which they have given me in the same manner.

This reveals that four of the children provided their mother, very probably on a monthly basis, with a minimum quantity of bread-grain and some fat. Certainly, it is less than Usekhnemte gave his father over a ten month period, but on the other hand it may have been adequate for an elderly lady. Moreover, it was not all Naunakhte received, for further on she records the landed property she had inherited from her first husband, a storeroom from her father, and the *oipe* of emmer which she collected together with her second husband. There is no doubt that she was not dependent upon the help of her children, but that was not a reason to forgive those who neglected their filial duties.

The Greek historian Herodotus describes in his *Histories* of *circa* 450 B.C., the various ways in which the Egyptians differed from other peoples. One of these is:

> It is not obligatory for the sons to feed their parents if they do not want to do so, but for daughters it is a strict obligation, even if they do not want it.

The 'father of history' is here not clear. As stated above, looking after and caring for one's parents is a moral duty, not enforceable in law. That the obligation was more stringent for girls than for boys is not confirmed by our source material.

In the late Papyrus Insinger (see p. 62), in a rather obscure passage, it seems to be stated that the obligation ceases if the parents behave like fools; then one is allowed to abandon them. Was that what Herodotus had in mind when he spoke about the sons? Or did he misunderstand his Egyptian informant, as was so many times the case?

That some children neglected their elderly parents we have seen. We could know that beforehand; it is only human. How many times it happened remains, of course, hidden. Actual life is hard to pinpoint. All we encounter are numerous examples of sons who want to be seen in their stereotyped inscriptions as virtuously caring for their ageing fathers and mothers.

X Old Age Pensions

In the preceding chapter we discussed the care of the elderly by their immediate family, especially the children. The question now arises as to whether the state looked after its servants in any particular fashion when they became too old to work. Of course, the state did not maintain <u>every</u> old person; such an old age pension is even in our society a recent development. But are there traces of a pension for those who were directly in the service of the state? Two possible groups emerge: the necropolis workmen at Thebes; and the soldiers and their commanding officers.

Dealing firstly with the former category, evidence occurs on a limestone ostracon now in Turin, dated to a particular month of year 7 of Ramesses II. The quantities of grain are recorded – both barley and emmer-wheat – which in that month were issued to the workmen and their chiefs. This grain constituted the basic wages. Among those who received it four women are mentioned. Perhaps they were simply the female slaves of the community who occur in many similar lists, but there they are always called "slaves". Alternatively, could the women here be the widows of deceased workmen?

This is not too bizarre a suggestion. In other such grain-distribution lists there occasionally occurs a person called a "widow". The incidences are unfortunately rare and not quite unambiguous. Yet, it seems possible that the authorities, who were responsible for the entire upkeep of these very special workers, also gave some food to their widows. Of course, we have no means of telling whether these ladies were elderly.

That older men among the builders of the Royal Tomb received a monthly grain-ration – lower than that of the ordinary workmen, but certainly still adequate – is proved by several of the grain-accounts. These men are explicitly called "old". Whether they still produced some work we do not know, but the payment seems to have been some sort of old age pension.

Of course, these people, the widows and the "old" men, were still partly dependent upon their family. The grain they received was merely a basic support, providing bread and beer.

That the state was responsible for the support of its soldiers is self-evident. In a world without money that had to be done by providing them with all they needed. An easier method was to allot to them pieces of land, together with cultivators. That system was widely followed, for instance, in Ptolemaic Egypt, but it was also customary in Pharaonic times. Soldiers were settled on the fields the government provided, while they could be called up for active service at every moment.

This is a payment, not a pension. If, however, the fields remained in the actual possession of the soldiers when they became too old to fight, then it almost became a pension. However, as we saw above (see p. 77), in some cases the obligations fell to the son, who acted as "staff of old age" for his father.

In the so-called *Miscellanies*, anthologies composed by teachers and used as schoolbooks during the New Kingdom, the desirable position of a scribe (that is, of an official) is contrasted with that of all other occupations.

One of the chapters describes the course of life of a common Egyptian:

> Man comes forth from the womb of his mother,
> and he runs to his master;
> the child is in the service of a soldier,
> the young man is a fighter,
> the old man is made to be a cultivator,
> the adult man to be a soldier.

"Old man" means here "veteran", as is explicitly the case in other similar texts. From the viewpoint of a scribe his fate is deplorable, but the reality behind it is that the veteran receives a field on the yield of which he stays alive, although he has to toil hard to do so.

Another *Miscellany* talks about various persons whom, says the author, one should not ridicule. One of them is a certain Amenwashu:

> Have you not heard the name of Amenwahsu, a veteran of the Treasury? He passed his life as a controller in the workshop beside the armoury.

It is not clear whether this passage refers to a former soldier or to a low level civil servant, who obtained a place in a workshop in order to keep himself alive. One can feel how the scribe looked down upon such a position. Yet, the old man Amenwahsu was not left to depend on the benevolence of his friends and family.

*Limestone statue of
Maya wearing the
'gold of honour'
(?Akhmim, Eighteenth
Dynasty). (Fig. 41)*

Above (see p. 64) we have quoted the Eighteenth Dynasty high
official Ineni. He receives daily, he tells us on the wall of his Theban
tomb, all kinds of food from the king's table. This also constitutes some
form of old age pension.

Another way of providing for elderly servants was that Pharaoh
appointed them to priestly offices. These positions may, in some cases,
have been no more than prebends, although some others seem to have
carried real duties.

As an example we can cite the soldier Maya, who served under
Tuthmosis III. He was buried in the 10th Upper Egyptian nome (later
called Antaiopolites), and it will be from there that the fine limestone
seated statue provenances, which is now in Berlin (fig. 41). Maya is here
depicted wearing a heavy double choker of gold ring beads, and four

100

armlets on both his wrists and upper arms. Those on his wrists are of a special type. All this jewellery constitutes the "gold of honour" with which kings of that period were wont to reward their gallant soldiers.

In what rank Maya served his sovereign he does not state. Apart from referring to the award he mentions on the seat of his statue only his later titles: "governor and chief of the prophets". It has been suggested that these are merely honorary designations, attached to sinecures, which were granted to him as an old age pension.

There are more examples of elderly soldiers who received such offices in the temples. A certain Amenemone, for instance, who lived at the very end of the Eighteenth Dynasty and was buried somewhere at Saqqara – the exact location has recently been rediscovered, and many elements from the tomb are now housed in museums all over the world – was first an army general. Later he was appointed steward of a funerary temple of Tuthmosis III, probably situated in Memphis. Whether this was a sinecure is not clear, however.

This is, by contrast, rather certain in the case of two former generals from the reign of Ramesses III. They are mentioned in the Great Harris Papyrus, the longest papyrus roll that has survived, being over 40 metres in length (see p. 68). Housed in the British Museum, it records the gifts donated by the king to various temples. In the last section, devoted to small temples, we come across a certain Inushefnu, "who had been a general" and was now in charge of a chapel of Rameses III in the temple of Min at Akhmim. Similarly, we read about a man named Dhutemhab, also a former general, who was in charge of a chapel in the temple of Wepwawet at Asyut. Little doubt exists that these two positions were prebends.

Less clear is the matter of a certain Amenhotep who was High Priest of Onuris, the local god of This, during the reign of Tuthmosis IV. On his stela, now also in the British Museum, he relates that he had been accustomed to accompany the ruler on his campaigns to Syro-Palestine and to Nubia. Probably this was in his capacity as stablemaster, that is, he was responsible for the horses of the chariotry. Hence, he was an army officer. When later appointed High Priest, he was in charge of the management and the finances of the temple, a position for which his work as chief of the royal stables may have prepared him. In how far his function was real or merely a sinecure is hard to establish, but it was certainly granted to him as a sort of pension. It should be noted that two of his sons, who are also represented on the stela, themselves became charioteers; evidently in the wake of their father's early employment.

Another High Priest of Onuris who enjoyed a similar career under the following dynasty is Anhermose (see p. 90), who lived under

Ramesses II and his successor Merneptah. His rock tomb at el-Mashayikh, the cemetery of ancient This, contains important wall reliefs which have recently been published (fig. 42).

According to his autobiographical inscriptions there, Anhermose started his career, after a very successful school education, as a military administrator in the chariotry corps. Later on he acted as "interpreter of every foreign land" for the king, and it was in this capacity that he attracted Pharaoh's attention. So he was introduced into the leading circles of the realm. This led, later in his life, to an appointment as High Priest of Onuris, although he was probably a Theban by birth. It may be that he even adapted his name to his new position, for Anhermose means "child of Onuris".

As regards his appointment, he relates how he was chosen by the god, which means singled out by an oracle from among a group of suitable persons put forward by the king. It was an administrative post, as we saw above; Anhermose himself assures us that he was not a ritual leader of the temple cult, but rather looked after the treasury and granaries of the temple.

Evidently, the function was bestowed on him as a reward for his loyal and efficient service to Pharaoh. In how far we should call it a pension office is not clear; but Anhermose also received a prebend of the same type as that of the two generals discussed above for he was steward of a chapel of Merneptah in the temple of Onuris.

That the transition from the army to the priesthood was not considered to be uncommon, even not to positions in the daily cult of the gods, is evident from the Coronation Decree of Horemhab. This text is written on the back of the diorite statue of Horemhab and his wife Mutnedjemet, now in Turin. The Pharaoh relates how he had set the land in order following the turmoil of the Amarna Period, rebuilding the temples that had fallen into disrepair, providing them with statues of the gods and regular offerings, endowing them with fields and herds, and equipping them with priests "from the pick of the army". Evidently, becoming a priest after serving as a soldier was not so exceptional as we would think.

Finally, mention can be made of the career of a certain Nebamun, known from the tomb he built in the Theban necropolis (TT 90). Originally he was standard-bearer of the ship called Meryamun ("Beloved of Amun"), which constituted a middle-rank military post. In his sixth regnal year Pharaoh Tuthmosis IV issued a palace decree, a copy of which is inscribed on one of the walls of the tomb. It was addressed to the commander of the fleet, a position not unlike that of the First Lord of the Admiralty, and it runs:

Anhermose dressed as High Priest (Tomb of Anhermose at el-Mashayikh, Nineteenth Dynasty). (Fig. 42)

My Majesty has ordered the receiving of a goodly old age, in the favour of the king, while care is taken of the standard-bearer Nebamun of the royal vessel Meryamun. He has reached old age while following Pharaoh in steadfastness, and being better today than yesterday, in performing what was put in his charge, without being reproached.

I have not found any fault in him, although he was accused as an offender. Now my Majesty has ordered to appoint him to be police chief on the West of the City (of Thebes), in the places Tembu and Obau, until he will reach the blessed state (of the dead).

This decree, together with the standard symbolizing the police force of Western Thebes, was handed over by a royal scribe called Iuny (fig. 43). Evidently, Nebamun received a pension position although it may not have been a sinecure. It should be noted that his brother was also a chief of police on the Theban West Bank. Clearly the king wished, now that Nebamun had been cleared from the accusations brought against him, that he should enjoy a quiet and well-provided for old age.

Nebamun (left) receives his appointment to police chief from the royal scribe Iuny (Tomb of Nebamun (TT 90), Eighteenth Dynasty). (Fig. 43)

Thus it appears evident that the government and Pharaoh himself looked after the elderly, especially former military men. How widespread this concern was we have no means of telling. Certainly, however, it did not extend to every old person in Ancient Egypt. The concept of an old age pension for every citizen was still millennia away.

XI Long-lived Kings

The age at which the Pharaohs died is generally unknown. All we can recognize is the number of years they ruled, or, rather, the highest year-date of these monarchs – which is not necessarily their last year. How old they were when they ascended the throne we can at best only estimate.

There are indications that the Egyptians believed that a king, when he became older, lost some of his magical potency, and that it was necessary to renew his forces. Such a renewal was the *sed*-festival (Egyptian: *Heb-sed*).

What the Egyptian word *sed* meant is unknown. In the Graeco-Roman Period the festival is called, as well in Demotic as in Greek, the "feast of thirty regnal years". The common rendering "jubilee" is not quite correct. Indeed, in most instances the ceremony took place in the thirtieth regnal year of a Pharaoh, after which it was regularly repeated every third year. At that moment most rulers would have been about fifty years old. Of Tuthmosis III we think that he was 46 years, of Amenhotep III that he was 47 years, while Ramesses II is considered to have been 55 years. This gives us an indication of the age at which, according to the Egyptians, a man became old. However, some rulers may have celebrated the festival at a far earlier moment in their life.

To establish which Pharaohs actually organized a *sed*-feast is far from easy. There are two reasons for this. Firstly, there are numerous mentions of what we might call "fictitious" celebrations: wishes to reach the date, which are so worded as to make it seem that it was already so far, or promises by the gods that it will be attained. Such expressions of wishes and promises created to the Egyptian mind the notion that it was already a reality. But this is not so according to our concepts.

Then, secondly, many texts and representations of the *sed*-festival actually refer to a celebration in the hereafter in which the ruler participated after his death. A clear example is the replica in stone of the temporary buildings erected for the feast, which are included in the complex of the Djoser-pyramid at Saqqara. To our mind these buildings,

King Neuserre carried in the Upper Egyptian palanquin (Sun-Temple of Neuserre at Abu Ghurab, Fifth Dynasty). (Fig. 44)

or scenes of the festival, which were particularly common during the Old Kingdom, constitute no proof that the pertinent king really celebrated the *Heb-sed*.

Our knowledge concerning the events of the festival is rather limited. There are no descriptions of the ceremonies, and only a few more extensive representations have survived. The earliest of these is found in the Fifth Dynasty Sun-Temple of King Neuserre at Abu Ghurab, North of Abusir. Originally two series of scenes existed, but of one of them sufficient has been preserved to venture a reconstruction (fig. 44). It should be noted that it is highly unlikely that Neuserre really celebrated his *Heb-sed*.

Some additional information has reached us from the reign of Amenhotep III, particularly from his temple at Soleb in Nubia (*circa* 200 kilometres South of Wadi Halfa). Unfortunately, however, its remains have not yet been adequately published. In the tombs of the high officials of this reign at Western Thebes, some scenes from the festival are also depicted, mainly those in which these persons themselves played a prominent rôle.

The third series dates from the early years of Amenhotep IV (the later Akhenaten). He built East of the Karnak Temple, outside the present enclosure wall, a structure which was specially devoted to his *Heb-sed*. After his reign the building was dismantled, and the blocks of the walls used to fill up the interior of some pylons in the Amun Temple. From here they have been recovered as a result of modern reconstruction work. These are the so-called *talatat*, perhaps named because their length is three times (three = Arabic: *talata*) that of a human hand.

The temple, called Gempaaten (literally "The Sun-disk is found") began to be excavated in the late seventies by a Canadian expedition. At the same time as its scanty remains were being exposed, an attempt was made to reconstruct the scenes on the *talatat*. From what we know at present of this building we can derive some information concerning the festival. Once again, it is dubious whether this Pharaoh indeed ever celebrated such a feast.

The last and perhaps most complete representation is found at Bubastis, in the Delta. In the temple there, Osorkon II, the most prominent ruler of the Twenty-Second Dynasty, erected a gateway decorated with scenes of the *Heb-sed*. Although more of these have survived than in the earlier cases, they too present only a partial picture of the events.

These four series of representations are vastly different. That is due, apart from their incomplete state of preservation, to the evolution of the *Heb-sed* over the centuries. The distance in time between Neuserre and the Amenhoteps is *circa* a thousand years, and that between the latter and Osorkon is again *circa* five hundred. No-one can expect the ceremony to have remained unchanged over such a stretch of time.

A few elements appear to have been characteristic for the festival. They occur also separately and outside the four series. But what is not depicted is the very beginning of the feast, namely, its announcement throughout the country sometime before. During the following months the divine statues of the temples were assembled and transported to the capital. This event is depicted in the tomb of a priest at el-Kab where a boat under sail is seen towing the sacred barge of Nekhbet, the goddess of this city, with the image of a deity in a shrine. The accompanying text tells us that in year 29 of Ramesses III the vizier was ordered to bring the goddess to the North. On the arrival in Ramsestown, in the Eastern Delta, the king himself came to take the front-hawser of the barque, a detail we know of only from this caption but which certainly conforms to reality.

For several days during the festival the ruler was seated on a throne in a pavilion, a scene which is depicted numerous times (fig. 45). He is shown once wearing the red crown of Lower Egypt and once with the white crown of Upper Egypt. In the representations these two are

Limestone lintel depicting the Sed-*Festival of Sesostris III (Temple of Montu at Medamud, Twelfth Dynasty). (Fig. 45)*

combined, the king being pictured twice, back-to-back. Generally, the actual ceremonies seem to have taken place twice, once for each part of the country.

During the rites the Pharaoh was clad in a special, enveloping cloak, which was conspicuously short, reaching to above the knees. The starched garment, which stood away from the neck, was decorated with coloured squares, and worn over a sort of feathered undergarment. In his hands he holds a staff and a whip. This attire is so characteristic that we can recognize statues in which the king is so represented (see fig. 47) as referring to his festival, either a real or a "fictitious" one. In later times, from Amenhotep III onwards, a longer, likewise all enveloping cloak replaces the earlier short version.

During the *Heb-sed* several processions took place, in which the Pharaoh was carried around in a palanquin. According to the scenes from both Abu Ghurab and the Gempaaten, the litter of the sovereign of

Upper Egypt was basket-shaped (see fig. 44), while that for Lower Egypt was square. The latter looks not unlike the famous carrying chair of Queen Hetepheres, the mother of Cheops, which is now in Cairo. The processions in which the king went around brought him to the temporary chapels in which the gods of all Egypt rested during those days, and where he brought his prayers and offerings.

A conspicuous rite, also many times depicted, is the so-called ceremonial course of the king, by which he asserted his dominance over the entire country. He is clearly running, probably between or around half-round constructions which are sometimes shown in the representations (fig. 46), and of which three-dimensional replicas can be seen in the Djoser complex. On this occasion, the king is not shown in the *Heb-sed* costume, but mostly in his habitual kilt. However, the course seems also to have been an element of ceremonies other than this festival.

Finally, the ceremonies contain allusions to a secret rite symbolizing the king's death and resurrection. In it a bed with lion's feet played a rôle, but exactly what is uncertain. Since the rite was obviously secret we possess no more than allusions as to what actually happened.

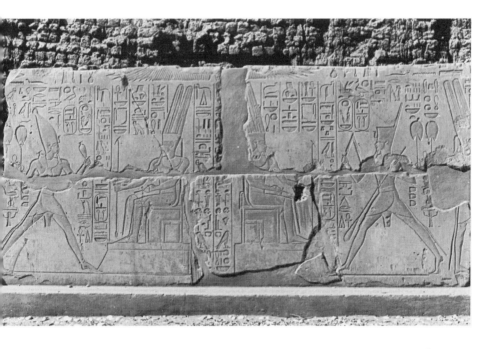

Limestone block depicting Amenhotep III running the ceremonial course before Amen-Re (Open Air Museum at Karnak, Eighteenth Dynasty). (Fig. 46)

In the past Egyptologists believed that the *Heb-sed* was a sort of civilized survival of a ritual that was supposed to have been common throughout Black Africa, during which a ruler, as soon as he displayed signs of becoming old and weak, was killed. However, no trace of this practice has ever been discovered in Egypt. Moreover, recent research has demonstrated that elsewhere in Africa such a ritual murder hardly occurred. Usually, it was executed in theory only, or a boy acted as substitute for the ruler. On the other hand, since it was believed that his magical potency, so necessary for the prosperity of his land and people, diminished, opponents of the government would use the opportunity to attempt to murder the king. That may also have happened in Egypt, as we shall see below.

In the shadow of this great state ceremony, simple daily life went on. That is aptly demonstrated by a text on a stela in the British Museum of a certain Nebipusenwosret, who played a rôle during the *sed*-festival of Amenemhat III in the Twelfth Dynasty. In the middle section, at the end of some biographical notes, we read that he made use of the opportunity presented by the presence of the priests of Osiris in the capital at the *Heb-sed* to send this stela with one of them back to Abydos, certainly in order to have it erected there.

How many Pharaohs really celebrated one or more *sed*-festivals we do not know, which is not a wonder in view of the complications mentioned above. A few doubtful instances may suffice to illustrate the problems.

That Amenhotep IV celebrated the feast in Thebes before his move to his new capital el-Amarna, which would mean, about his third regnal year, is doubtful despite the building of Gempaaten. It would have been excessively early in his reign. On the other hand, the features of the king and the queen in the representations on the *talatat* were not exaggerated as they subsequently became in later years, which proves that the scenes indeed date from early in his reign. It has been suggested that he celebrated the feast together with his father, whose third *sed*-festival in his regnal year 37 is certain. But for this hypothesis there exists no positive proof at all.

A much discussed problem is that of Hatshepsut's festival. Her own reign was certainly not long enough for her to have celebrated a thirty-year festival, but it has been suggested that she counted, not from her own accession, but from that of her father Tuthmosis I. There are indeed vague indications of a *Heb-sed* in her regnal year 16, but definitive proof is as yet lacking.

We can only be certain that the festival took place if, for instance, dated records of its proclamation have been preserved, or dated dockets on jars in which the food for the feast was sent to the capital; or also when we possess mentions of the date of a second or third celebration. Without such evidence the actuality of the event remains doubtful.

At present only a dozen instances are fairly or quite certain. That means that for several kings, of whom we know for certain that their reign lasted for more than thirty years, no proof of a *Heb-sed* is available. An example of these is Amenemhat II, whose rule lasted at least thirty-five years. This silence may mean that, for whatever reason, no *sed*-feast was held; it may equally well be due to a lacuna in our documentation. This is less strange than it might seem to be. Of the so well-known Pharaoh Amenhotep III, for instance, we possess not a single

Calcite (Egyptian alabaster) statuette of Pepy I (Saqqara, Sixth Dynasty). (Fig. 47)

111

Limestone statue of Montuhotep II Nebhetepre in his Heb-sed *garb (Causeway of the Montuhotep Temple at Deir el-Bahri, Eleventh Dynasty). (Fig. 48)*

text dated between his regnal years 11 and 30, and hardly any private documents from this period.

One point is clear: the *sed*-festival sheds light on the Egyptian conceptions of what was needed by an ageing Pharaoh. By the extensive ceremonies his power over the country and its inhabitants was renewed.

Let us now discuss some of the kings of whom we know, from their *Heb-sed* or other evidence, that they enjoyed a long-lasting reign. The earliest king of whom it is rather certain that he celebrated *sed*-festivals, and who may therefore have enjoyed a long reign, was Qa'a, the last ruler of the First Dynasty. This is almost all, however, that we know of him. He seems to have reigned only sixteen years, which rather contradicts the suggestion of a long reign. If this is correct, it may be that a *sed*-festival in those early days was not yet celebrated in the thirtieth regnal year.

That Qa'a indeed reached his *Heb-sed*, and even his second, appears evident from the inscription on a sherd from a schist bowl found in Djoser's Step Pyramid. The words: "second time of *Heb-sed*" are clear; admittedly, the name of the Pharaoh has almost totally broken off, but the slight traces fit this name among those of the early Pharaohs.

Qa'a was buried in Umm el-Qa'ab, the cemetery of the early kings on the hills above Abydos. There his tomb, from which no clearly dated material is known, was surrounded by the subsidiary graves of his retainers. One of the mastabas excavated by Walter Bryan Emery at Saqqara in 1953, which has been ascribed to Qa'a, was probably simply the burial place of one of his officials. More we cannot tell about him; the first long-lived king remains a shadowy figure to us.

The next ruler, for which our evidence decisively suggests that he reigned into old age, is Pepi I, from the Sixth Dynasty. He certainly celebrated a *sed*-festival, as is proved not only by a statue in ceremonial dress now in Brooklyn (fig. 47), on the base of which the words "first time of the *Heb-sed*" are incised, but also by some rock inscriptions in the Wadi Hammamat. Three of them also mention the "first time" of the *sed*-festival, but the fourth explicitly states: "Year of the 18th occasion, third month of the third season, day 27: first time of the *Heb-sed*".

The date requires an explanation. In the Old Kingdom the years were not yet reckoned after the regnal years of the king, as in later times, but after a two-yearly census of oxen and small cattle. Hence they were called: "Year of the x-th occasion" (of the counting), or "Year after the x-th occasion". This would mean that the "Year of the 18th occasion" of Pepi I was his regnal year 36. However, it is not certain that the census always took place every second year. Actually, we know that this was not the case; it could happen in two (or more?) successive years. So we cannot be sure about the date of this *Heb-sed*. It may be that it was celebrated earlier, perhaps in Pepi's thirtieth year.

In the Wadi Magharah, in the Sinai, a tablet has been found dated to the "Year after the 18th occasion". The text lists the names of the expedition leaders of that year. At the top are two scenes: one shows the king smiting his enemies, the other depicts the ceremonial course. The latter suggests that a *sed*-festival really took place around this time.

Regnal year 36 or 37, if that was indeed meant, is not the highest date we know of for Pepi I. An inscription in the alabaster quarries of Hatnub, near el-Amarna, makes mention of "King Meryre" (the *prenomen* of Pepi) and of "the 25th occasion". That could mean that he reigned for at least fifty years. Even if he came to the throne at an early age, he was evidently a long-lived Pharaoh.

Pepi I's reign is considered to be the culmination point of the Old Kingdom. Throughout the country evidence of his building activities have been found. The name of his pyramid at Saqqara, *Mn-nfr-Ppi* ("The Beauty of Pepi endures"), was later used to indicate the nearby capital in the form Memphis. For all his deeds, including expeditions into the desert, he had clearly sufficient time in his long reign, even if it lasted somewhat less than half a century.

Pepi's son Merenre reigned only a few years, and was succeeded, after his untimely death, by his half-brother Pepi II, the son of Pepi I's second wife (see p. 78). First his mother acted as regent, together with her brother Djau, for Pepi was still a child. The famous and exquisite statue of Egyptian alabaster in the Brooklyn Museum, showing him, with full regalia, sitting on the lap of his mother, reflects this situation.

The later tradition attests that Pepi came to the throne in his sixth year, and that he reigned till he was a hundred years old. This seems hardly likely; it sounds too much like the ideal lifetime (see Chapter 6). Yet, he was certainly one of the longest reigning Pharaohs.

A graffito in his pyramid temple at Saqqara South is dated to "the 31st occasion". It records a ritually correct burial. Whether it refers to the entombment of the king is not clear. If it was that, then he would have reigned over sixty years, but this has to remain hypothetical.

Of course, Pepi II celebrated *sed*-festivals. A rock inscription at Elephantine mentions the second, but without a date. Also, some names of officials are composed with the words *Heb-sed*, such as that of the Vizier Ni-heb-sed-Neferkare (Neferkare: Pepi's *prenomen*). Yet, all this is less than one would expect from such a long reign. There is no inscription of the monarch from his later years. In that period the dissolution of the state began, which would soon afterwards lead to the collapse of the Old Kingdom. In how far the advanced age of Pepi II was a factor in this process we have no means of telling.

From the Middle Kingdom the evidence concerning long-lived kings is more extensive. It begins with the Eleventh Dynasty ruler Montuhotep II Nebhepetre, who reunited Egypt after the First Intermediate Period. He reigned at least forty-six years, and certainly celebrated a *Heb-sed*, but in what regnal year is uncertain. Perhaps it was in his year 39. In the Wadi Shatt er-Rigal, near the relief mentioned above (see p. 80 and fig. 33), there is another representation of the monarch, this time in the garment of the *sed*-festival. Beside it there is written: "39th regnal year", but it is not quite certain that this refers to the feast. Several statues have been found in the ceremonial garb, some of which were erected along the causeway to his mortuary temple at Deir el-Bahri (fig. 48). Unfortunately, none of them bears a dated inscription.

It is uncertain in which year Montuhotep defeated the Herakleopolitans and reunified Egypt. Some scholars would like to see a connection between these events and the change of the king's Horus name, first from Seankhtawi to Netjerhedjet, and later to Sematawi ("He who Unites the Two Lands"). The last name would have been used from the moment that unity was restored, perhaps from year 30 onwards, while the first change is connected with the defeat of the Tenth Dynasty, after regnal year 14. That is, however, rather speculative. On the other hand, it is certain that Montuhotep Nebhepetre belongs to the long-lived Pharaohs.

The first sovereign of the Twelfth Dynasty was Amenemhat I. It has been suggested that he was previously the Vizier under Montuhotep IV, the last Pharaoh of the Eleventh Dynasty, but that is no more than a possibility. The name was a common one in the Theban area. We possess no information on how he gained power.

Amenemhat reigned until his twenty-ninth year. From the famous *Story of Sinuhe* we know that on a day in year 30 he was murdered, probably during the preparations for his first *sed*-festival. Whether his opponents objected to the rise of the new dynasty is uncertain, but if that was the case they were unsuccessful. The crown-prince Sesostris, who was on an expedition to the Western desert – conceivably in order to collect cattle for the feast – rushed back to the capital and seized power. That the moment for the attack on the king had to do with his supposed weakness before his potency was renewed by the ritual is well possible.

A famous literary composition from these days is the so-called *Instruction of Amenemhat for his Son*. It was written by a royal scribe in the early years of Sesostris I, but it well expresses the disappointment of the father in his friends:

> Do not trust a brother, know no friend,
> make no intimates, it is worthless.
> When you lie down, guard your heart (that is, your life) yourself,
> for no man has adherents on the day of woe.

Sesostris I reigned for forty-five years, but only one *sed*-festival of his is known. Its date, year 31 (without a month or day) occurs in a graffito at Hatnub, belonging to a certain nomarch called Amenemhat, son of Nehri. He relates how he came to the quarry in order to fetch stone for the monarch. There are also undated references to a first *Heb-sed*, for instance on the beautiful White Chapel of the king at

Karnak, now rebuilt in the Open Air Museum there. However, such casual mentions are in themselves no proof that the feast actually took place. Of later celebrations we do not hear anything, although the reign certainly lasted long enough for them to have taken place.

The time of Sesostris I seems to have been far from peaceful. His foreign policy was mainly directed to the conquest of Nubia and the defence against the Kingdom of Kerma, South of the third cataract. All this does not give the impression that he particularly needed to renew his forces in his later years, even though he must have become old in Egyptian eyes. Anyhow, we merely hear about a *Heb-sed* in his year 31. Why not in year 30 is a mystery.

As already stated above (see p. 111), we know of no *sed*-festival under Amenemhat II, despite a reign of thirty-five years. Generally, there is not much information on this period. Yet, one of the titles of a nomarch called Khnumhotep, found in his tomb at Beni Hasan and which relates to his appointment as governor over a sub-nome in regnal year 17, may perhaps point to the feast. It contains an unknown word, written three times with a half-round sign that resembles the object between which the king was running during the ceremonial course (see p. 109 and fig. 46). That is all the indication we have for a possible *Heb-sed*.

The next two Pharaohs, Sesostris II and III, reigned for too short a time to have celebrated the festival, namely twelve and *circa* twenty years respectively. Nevertheless, the latter is depicted in his ceremonial dress sitting in the pavilion, once with the red and once with the white crown. The scene occurs on a lintel from the Temple of Medamud (see fig. 45), which is now in the Cairo Museum. The gods of the two halves of the country, Horus and Seth, hand over to him the symbol of the festival. This is one of the numerous "fictitious" representations.

Finally, the last great Pharaoh of the Twelfth Dynasty, Amenemhat III, reigned for over forty-five years. The documentation on his *Heb-sed* – only one is attested – is scanty. In the round top of a stela belonging to a certain Seniankh, which was found at Naga ed-Deir, the date is given as "Year 30 under the Majesty of Nimaatre" (the *prenomen* of Amenemhat III). In a different hand there was later added, in small signs and lightly incised: "*Heb-sed*". And on a stela now in the British Museum a certain Nebipusenwosret relates that he took part in the celebration of a *sed*-festival, but without mention of a date. That is all, apart from some representations and aspirations; there is no royal inscription recording the feast.

The reign of Amenemhat was peaceful. It was characterized by a large number of expeditions, to the Sinai and other places in the Eastern desert, but not by many military actions. Why this Pharaoh celebrated no

Limestone unfinished triad recently identified as Amenhotep III, Teye, and Beketaten (el-Amarna, Eighteenth Dynasty). (Fig. 49)

more *sed*-festivals is a riddle. Did he think that his health was so good that he did not need to renew his magical potency? Or is this yet another example of our lacunary documentation? At present no satisfactory answer is forthcoming.

Four kings of the New Kingdom reigned sufficiently long to reach the time for a *Heb-sed*. The first one of these is Tuthmosis III. He succeeded his father when he was still a young child, while his aunt Hatshepsut, the widow of Tuthmosis II and daughter of Tuthmosis I, acted as regent. Some years later she herself ascended the throne,

117

without ever deposing her nephew, who also became her son-in-law. During his youth it was Hatshepsut who held sway, although formally they reigned together. Whether she actually celebrated a *sed*-festival is not clear (see p. 110).

In Tuthmosis' regnal year 22 she disappears; how, and why at that particular point, we do not know. Immediately, the king started on the first of his many military campaigns into Syro-Palestine, which led to the famous Battle of Megiddo. In total he would lead his victorious army sixteen times into the field, the last in his year 42. On account of these exploits he is sometimes referred to as "the Napoleon of Antiquity".

In between his various expeditions Tuthmosis found the time to celebrate at least three *sed*-festivals. The third one is mentioned on one of the faces of the erroneously named Cleopatra's needle, the obelisk in London on the Embankment. Originally, it was erected at Heliopolis, together with its companion which now stands behind the Metropolitan Museum of Art, in Central Park in New York. They were placed before the Temple of Re on the occasion of the monarch's third *Heb-sed*. Under the Emperor Augustus they were transported to Alexandria, from where one came to London in 1878, the other to New York in 1881.

There is little evidence for Tuthmosis' *sed*-festivals. A stela at el-Bersheh, from year 33, mentions "the beginning of millions of very many *Heb-seds*", which is usually connected with the second occasion. No date is known for the third, and later ones, if they ever took place, have left us without any documentation. Yet, Tuthmosis reigned for fifty-four years, long enough to have celebrated more of these feasts. At his death he would have been nearing his sixty-fifth year, so he was according to Egyptian concepts certainly long-lived.

The second Eighteenth Dynasty Pharaoh we will discuss is Amenhotep III, "the Dazzling Sun-Disk". He came to the throne as a child of eight or ten years. Therefore, during his first regnal years the country was governed by his mother Mutemwia, a minor wife of his father Tuthmosis IV, who was ruling with the help of others. Among these may have been the commander of the chariotry Yuya (see p. 85), whose daughter Teye would eventually become Amenhotep's wife.

For the king's three *sed*-festivals fairly extensive documentation exists, particularly in the Soleb Temple, at Karnak (see fig. 46), and in the Theban monuments of some of his high officials. For instance, Amenhotep, son of Hapu, a military officer, mentions in his funerary temple that he was appointed, at the end of the first *Heb-sed* in year 30, to a honorary office, indicated by an archaic title which may literally mean "canal-digger". Nefersekheru, the steward of the royal palace at Malkata, in Western Thebes (in the vicinity of Medinet Habu), where all three festivals were celebrated, depicted in his tomb (TT 107) some of the scenes in which he played a rôle. So too did the steward of the queen, Kheruef (TT 192). All this would not yet be a decisive proof for the feasts having taken place, but from the many hundreds of jar-dockets found littering the site at Malkata they become a certainty. These are the dated inscriptions on the vessels in which the provisions for the banquets held during the feasts were sent to the palace.

When the king died, shortly after his third festival, he was not yet fifty years of age; to our concepts not yet an old man. Even so, he is depicted in his later years as elderly (fig. 49), which may have been due to a fatal disease. He was succeeded by his son Amenhotep IV, who soon took the name Akhenaten and launched a violent and systematic attack on the traditional divinities of Egypt. Although, as related above, he built a temple for his *sed*-feast at Karnak, it is doubtful whether he actually celebrated it (see p. 107).

The longest-living Pharaoh of the entire history of Ancient Egypt was Ramesses II. His lengthy reign as well as his achievements made a lasting impression on his successors. On a stela from his year 4 at Abydos, which is dedicated to Osiris, Ramesses IV declares: "You (the god) shall double for me the long lifespan and lengthy kingship of King Usimare-Stepenre (that is, Ramesses II), the Great God. Indeed, more numerous are the deeds and benefactions which I have done for your temple in order to supply your sacred offerings ...... in these four years than what King Usimare-Stepenre, the Great God, did for you in his sixty-seven years". These words clearly demonstrate the awe and wonder in which the later Pharaohs looked back to their great predecessor.

In accordance with his long reign Ramesses II celebrated more *sed*-festivals than any other king, namely fourteen; although the last one was perhaps only announced and never actually took place. They started in his regnal year 30, and were then regularly repeated every three or four years. Curiously enough, we have no representations of any of these feasts, nor statues of the king in festive attire, although Ramesses II has generally left us with numerous attestations of his many years. All we know about these occasions is that they were announced; the first five by his son Khaemwaset (see pp. 133-135 and fig. 54) and a vizier, the remainder by a vizier alone. The inscriptions recording the announcements have survived at several sites in Upper Egypt, but for some unknown reason not in Lower Egypt.

Since Ramesses was not a child any more when he ascended the throne – he would have been at least twenty-five years old – he must have lived until he was over ninety. He is famous (or perhaps rather infamous) for the number of children he fathered: fifty-two sons and forty daughters,

Ramesses III: (a) face of granite standard-bearing statue (Karnak cachette, Twentieth Dynasty); (b) head of his mummy (Deir el-Bahri cache, Twentieth Dynasty). (Fig. 50)

produced, not surprisingly with various wives. The most important of these was Nefertari, the first consort, to whom the smaller temple at Abu Simbel was dedicated, and then Isinofre, the mother of Ramesses' beloved daughter Bentanat and the princes Ramesses, Khaemwaset, and Merneptah. It was the latter, son number thirteen, who would eventually succeed his father. Some of the sons, for instance Khaemwaset, had already acted for some years as regents, for it appears that the king, when he became old, was not capable of ruling any more himself.

Ramesses would not have been the only Pharaoh to have had such an extensive family, yet none of the others lays such a stress on his offspring. In this respect, as in many others, he was evidently an unusual monarch, whose era saw the last flowering of Egyptian history.

The final Pharaoh of the New Kingdom to have occupied the throne for a considerable length of time was Ramesses III. Although he too ascended when he was not so young any more, perhaps in his early thirties (fig. 50a), he reigned for just over thirty-two years. His first *Heb-sed* was celebrated, as we would expect, in his regnal year 30. There is not much documentation to support this fact, but in an administrative papyrus in Turin we come across the remark that in year 29 the Vizier passed Thebes to the North in order to bring the gods of Upper Egypt to the feast.

In his year 32 Ramesses would have started the preparations for his second *Heb-sed*. At that time, a conspiracy centred in the Royal Harim took place. In this a minor queen and her son, together with several court officials and high dignitaries, devised a plot to murder the Pharaoh while he visited Thebes to take part in a religious festival. Whether the attack met with complete success is not clear, but soon afterwards, Ramesses "flew up to heaven", perhaps as a result of the attempt, although his famous mummy shows no trace of any wound (fig. 50b). Probably, the conspirators hoped to make use of the king's loss of magical powers during the month before the renewal of the *sed*-ceremonies, as was the case with Amenemhat I. They too met with no success, for once again it was the crown-prince, this time Ramesses IV, who seized control.

It is conspicuous that, according to the papyri recording the conviction of the culprits, they had tried to use magic. This confirms the suggestion that they considered the ruler to be weak and vulnerable. Whether there was a political motif we have no means of knowing; certainly, no text makes any mention of it. That rivalry in the harim played a vital part is no more than a plausible hypothesis.

One of the most extensive sources for the events during a *sed*-festival are the representations on a gateway in the temple of the cat goddess Bastet at Bubastis (see p. 107). This structure was erected by King Osorkon II in his regnal year 22, and the text in which this is stated appears to be an exact replica of that of Amenhotep III on his festival monument at Soleb. That in itself is sufficient reason to doubt whether the feast ever occurred at this date. Other evidence that could prove the reality is absent.

So our series must end as it began with Qa'a (and Neuserre), namely, with a query-mark. Did this *Heb-sed* ever really take place? What could have been the clearest proof of a long reign for Osorkon II is actually not clear at all. As we have seen, to distinguish between fact and fiction is not always so easy.

XII Aged Administrators

In this chapter our aim is to present to the reader some elderly officials at various levels of Egyptian society. Of course, the number of aged statesmen and executives from whom we could choose is boundless. Actually, almost everyone who became powerful enough to leave monuments, whether stelae, statues, or tombs, would have been older, although we seldom know exactly how old.

A Pepiankh-the-Middle, a nomarch and priest of Hathor from Meir, who flourished in the time of Pepi II, wrote in his autobiography on the wall of his tomb: "I spent the time till a hundred years among the honoured living ones in possession of my *ka* (i.e. well provided for). I spent a great part of this time as chief priest of Hathor ...... to see her and to perform her ceremonial with my hands". In giving us a figure Pepiankh is an exception, but that these "hundred years" refer to reality is more than doubtful (see Chapter 6).

From all the numerous possible aged administrators we have chosen a few concerning whom something more can be said than that they simply became old and attained a high position. Each of them represents a particular facet of Ancient Egyptian civilization, so that this last chapter also offers the reader a range of views on life in those times. Our elderly subjects will be discussed in chronological order.

Our first choice is Hemiunu, Vizier and Overseer of all Works of the Pharaoh Khufu. This means that he was responsible for the construction of the Great Pyramid, the largest of all pyramids on the Giza plateau. He was the son of Nefermaat, who was also his predecessor as Vizier, a royal prince whose impressive mastaba was situated near the pyramid of Meidum. Since this was the burial place of Huni, the last ruler of the Third Dynasty, it may be that Nefermaat was his son. Anyhow, Hemiunu certainly belonged to the royal family without actually being the son of a Pharaoh. When he is called "son of the king of his body", this is purely an honorific title.

In the early Old Kingdom the viziers were taken from the sons of Pharaoh. Only his own children possessed sufficient magical powers to represent their father. In the Fourth Dynasty the circle from which they were recruited was enlarged, but still restricted to blood relations of the king. That may be the reason why the famous Imhotep, the builder of the Step Pyramid at Saqqara, never became a vizier: he was merely a commoner.

The power concentrated in the hands of these early viziers such as Hemiunu (see p.14) was considerable. He was head of the entire administration of the state, responsible for the building works on temples and the royal funerary complex, for which he had the authority to call up *corvée* workers throughout the country. He was director of the state finances; organizer of expeditions into the deserts and to foreign countries; in fact, only the supervision over the temples and over military affairs remained exclusively in the hands of Pharaoh himself.

That he was such a heavy-weight in the state is reflected by Hemiunu's lifesize seated statue which was found in his tomb in the Western Field of Giza, and is now in Hildesheim (fig. 51). The tomb itself

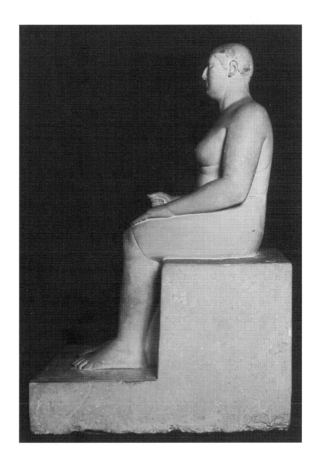

Limestone statue of the elderly Vizier Hemiunu (Mastaba of Hemiunu at Giza, Fourth Dynasty). (Fig. 51)

is one of the largest in this area (*circa* 53 by 27 metres), which is in accordance with Hemiunu's position. The limestone statue was discovered by Junker in 1912 in a small, closed room, a so-called *serdab* (Arabic for "cellar"), behind one of the false doors. Tomb robbers had entered it in antiquity and broken off the head, which was found almost intact at its feet; only a small fragment was lost and had to be restored. The eyes, however, made of crystal and affixed with gold, had been wantonly smashed from their settings.

When found the statue still presented traces of its original colouring: black hair and a red-brown body. It shows an aristocratic type of man, in what was then a novel attitude: both hands on the legs, in contrast to the preceding style in which the subject held one hand before his breast. The corpulent body, indubitably a realistic trait, denoted the elderly administrator. In its monumental pose it can certainly claim to be one of the masterpieces of Old Kingdom art. Standing before it in the Pelizaeus Museum, one can easily conjure up the power and authority of this aged statesman.

What we know about our second subject, Uni, is of a totally different nature. Certainly, he too became an elderly statesman, for he served under three Sixth Dynasty Pharaohs: Teti, Pepi I, and Merenre. That means that he must have lived for over sixty years at the most conservative estimate. His fame in Egyptology he acquired by his autobiography, inscribed on the wall of his tomb-chapel at Abydos (now in the Cairo Museum), where it was discovered by Auguste Mariette, then Director of Egyptian Monuments, in 1860. The text is of a highly literary character, with rhythmic and poetic features, and contains reminiscences of the famous Pyramid Texts. Sentences of it were copied in a composition on a statue from the Twenty-Sixth Dynasty, demonstrating that the Egyptians themselves recognized its literary calibre. Yet, it certainly relates real history.

Uni, who is actually called in several texts Uni-the-Elder, probably because he had a son of the same name, enjoyed an exceptional career. He started in the palace administration, where he quickly gained the confidence of the king. He requested and acquired permission to bring from the Tura quarries, some kilometres South of Cairo, a white limestone sarcophagus and a false-door with its lintel, two door-jambs, and a libation-table, to be placed in his mastaba. The sarcophagus is now lost, but the false-door was found in the tomb and is also now in the Cairo Museum.

A decisive moment in Uni's career came when a plot was discovered in the harim in which the Royal Consort was involved. It was Uni who, on order of the Pharaoh, alone acted as judge, without any colleague, even the

Vizier, although it was with a high juridical executive that the official report was drawn up. That Uni was allowed to hear the secrets of the harim was a clear proof of trust and appreciation on the part of the king.

Then, he was placed at the head of a large army, assembled from all over Egypt, and which included Nubian mercenaries. At that time Egypt did not possess a standing army nor a professional officer corps; local administrators (the nomarchs) commanded the contingents of their districts, while Uni, although certainly no military man, devised the plans and supervised the organization.

The action culminated in the defeat of the "Sand-dwellers", as the inhabitants of Syro-Palestine are here called. Although it literally indicates Bedouin, it is used in this text in a wider sense. A hymn in the autobiography describes the victorious return of the troops:

> This army returned in peace,
>> after having razed the land of the Sand-dwellers.
> This army returned in peace,
>> after having ravaged the land of the Sand-dwellers.
> This army returned in peace,
>> after having attacked its strongholds.
> This army returned in peace,
>> after having cut down its figs and vines. ......

Notwithstanding the triumph, Uni had to be sent five times, since the unruly Sand-dwellers revolted time and time again. Once he employed a conspicuous ruse. He transported half his troops by ship along the Mediterranean coast, landing them behind the enemy lines, while the remainder of the army proceeded over the road. So encircling his opponents, he crushed them and killed them all.

Rising yet higher in the administration, Uni was appointed to the position of governor of all Upper Egypt, from somewhat South of Memphis to the border at Elephantine. He was sent to Nubia to fetch a sarcophagus for Pharaoh Merenre and a pyramidion for his pyramid. The sarcophagus, a grey diorite monolith, has indeed been found in the tomb of this king at Saqqara South. On another occasion Uni journeyed to Elephantine for a granite false-door, a libation-stone, lintels, and other elements of Merenre's pyramid. Yet another expedition went to Hatnub, to fetch a great altar of alabaster. For its transport, he had built a barge of acacia wood, and he succeeded in delivering the altar in a record seventeen days, despite the fact, as he tells us, that it was summer and there was no water on the sandbanks.

So Uni received one charge after another, performing each and every one in an exemplary fashion. Clearly, we see in Uni one of the most successful aged administrators of the Old Kingdom.

Our third man, Rediu-Khnum of the Eleventh Dynasty, occupied a more modest position, although the tone of his autobiography would perhaps suggest otherwise. The text is written on a large rectangular stela, 152 by 62 centimetres, originally erected in his tomb at Dendera, and now in the Cairo Museum. At the bottom Rediu-Khnum himself is depicted, seated before a huge amount of offerings, with his pet dog under his seat and the small figure of the butler under the food.

All this is not exceptional, and neither is the text of twenty-three lines, although it differs completely from the factual, well-worded biography of Uni. Beginning with the traditional offering formula, Redi-Khnum continues with a string of high-flown epithets in which he describes himself as, for example:

> ...... efficient in performance at every task,
> dignified, open-handed, pleasant mannered,
> white-robed, handsome, godly to behold ......

Such phrases do not really tell us anything about the man himself. As in most autobiographies of the Middle Kingdom, the text is more naive than we can appreciate. Confined within the funerary context – the stela stood in a tomb – it uses shameless *clichés*, stressing the code of moral behaviour instead of describing an individual life.

Yet, within this context, we can elicit some hard facts. Redi-Khnum states that he was:

> His lady's confidant whom she favours,
> whom she placed in the great estate ......
> I have spent a long time of years under my mistress,
> the Royal Ornament Nefrukayet ......
> foremost noblewoman of this land,
> foremost nobility of Upper Egypt,
> being a king's daughter and a king's beloved wife,
> and having inherited from all her mothers.

Who was this royal lady whom Redi-Khnum served? Very probably she is to be identified as the wife of Wahankh Antef II and the mother of Antef III, both rulers of the Eleventh Dynasty. In other texts she is referred to by the abbreviation Nefru. That she was a mighty personality in those days appears evident from the following lines:

She resettled Upper Egypt, the van of men,
from Elephantine to the Antaiopolite nome,
(that is, the tenth Upper Egyptian nome),
with women together with managers and officials
from the entire land.

Rediu-Khnum passed "a long time, a span of many years" in the service of his mistress, so that it can be suggested that he was elderly when he erected the stela. Of course, he was "without there being any fault of mine, for my competence was great". In real life he was placed at the head of the Queen's estate at Dendera, a cattle farm she had inherited from her mother, and which Rediu-Khnum claims was "the greatest estate of Upper Egypt". Even if we take this with a pinch of salt, it is clear that Rediu-Khnum was a competent administrator in the period shortly before the reunification of the country under Montuhotep II Nebhepetre (see p. 80 and 114). It may be noted in passing that the plethora of modern studies on women in Ancient Egypt have as yet neglected the queen of this text, although she clearly seems worthy of some attention!

Rather more eminent than this local official is our next subject, who was called Ikhernofret. He was the owner of a chapel at Abydos in which not only the main stela which we will discuss was erected, but also, as was usual in Abydene tomb-chapels, the stelae of a number of his colleagues and subordinates. The chapel itself has long been destroyed, but we present here a possible reconstruction of such structures (fig. 52). Its elements have been dispersed over several Egyptological collections all over the world. That they originally belonged together is proved by the mention of Ikhernofret's name and titles on most of them. One even states explicitly that it was made for this particular tomb-chapel.

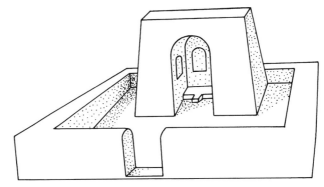

Diagram of a reconstructed chapel (Abydos, Middle Kingdom). (Fig. 52)

Limestone stela of Ikhernofret framed by a raised border (Tomb-chapel of Ikhernofret at Abydos, Twelfth Dynasty). (Fig. 53)

The stelae are mostly undated, but one of them is from year 1 of Amenemhat III, while the main one bears the names and titles of Sesostris III. Most revealing is a sentence at the bottom of a third one, now in Geneva, which states that the chamberlain Sisetyt, the son of the owner, went with Ikhernofret to the festival of Osiris, on order of Pharaoh Sesostris III, "when he threw down the vile Kush in regnal year 19". From other sources we know that Sesostris indeed campaigned that year in Nubia. So it is clear when the events described below exactly took place.

The round-topped limestone stela, measuring 100 by 65 centi-metres and including a raised border, is now in Berlin (fig. 53). Since the text is one of the very few that informs us about the Osiris festival at Abydos, generally known as the Osiris mysteries, it has been the subject of several studies, although much still remains obscure. It begins with the king's command to the Overseer of the Treasury Ikhernofret – probably using the actual words of Pharaoh's letter – to go to Abydos and make monuments for Osiris Khentamenti (that is, "Foremost of the Westerners", the local name of this deity), and to adorn his sacred image with the fine gold which Sesostris had recently brought back from his victorious campaigns in Nubia.

The king gave this commission to Ikhernofret because, as the letter states, he trusted him, for he had grown up as a foster-son of the king. When he was twenty-six years old he had been made a "Companion", a favoured courtier in the inner circle. "Now" – that is, evidently years later, which implies that he was not any more young – he is sent to perform this significant task.

He served Osiris, in accordance with his Majesty's command, as a "beloved son", a function derived from the family cult in which the eldest son acted as priest for his deceased parent. He renewed the palanquin in which the god would be carried around during the procession, with gold, silver, lapis lazuli, bronze, and costly wood. He also embellished the cult statue and clothed it in its regalia, and rearranged the priestly service in the temple.

So much for the first part of the text, which is followed by a report on the processions. Unfortunately, since we do not know what exactly happened and as the Egyptian words are not always clear, there needs remains a great deal of guesswork. First, as a prelude, there was a procession of Wepwawet ("Way-Opener"), a local jackal deity who was identified with Horus, for he is said "to rescue his father". It seems that a fight took place, either symbolic or actual, for Ikhernofret says: "I repulsed the attackers of the *neshmet*-barque (on which the Osiris statue was carried) and I felled the foes of Osiris". Evidently, the (deceased) god-king also took part in the ceremonial journey.

Then followed the "Great Procession", which was actually the funeral cortège of the god. His boat is said to have sailed, but whether it indeed went over water is uncertain since the journey ended in Peqer, that is Umm el-Qaʿab (see p. 113), in the desert West of Abydos, and that could not be reached over water. Once again there is reference to a "great combat" in which all the enemies of Osiris fell. Then, what may be a rite connected with the burial and resurrection of the god is alluded to, but only vaguely since this was a secret mystery. At the end, the *neshmet*-barque was brought back, to the accompaniment of cheers, to "his palace". Ikhernofret followed the god to his house, that is, the Abydos Temple, where he came to rest.

This fascinating text has made Ikhernofret's name famous in the annals of Egyptology, even though we only partially understand what really occurred. Whatever he did in his function as Overseer of the

Treasury – he does not tell us one thing about it – this particular commission was evidently the culmination point in the career of this aged administrator.

Proceeding to the Eighteenth Dynasty, we could mention a large number of elderly statesmen, several of whom have already found a place in one of the preceding chapters. There are, for instance, Senenmut, the *éminence grise* of Hatshepsut (see p. 81), and Amenhotep, son of Hapu, the favourite of King Amenhotep III (see pp. 61 and 76), or also Amenemhat, the High Priest of Amun, who was the son of a simple artisan and remained an ordinary priest, until at the age of fifty-four he suddenly rose to this elevated position (see p. 76). Finally, there is Ay, the distinguished statesman of the Amarna Period, who ended up as Pharaoh after the untimely death of Tutankhamun (see p. 85). All these aged administrators are well-known, and sufficient has been said of them above and also in the literature in general.

Instead, we prefer to present here a less famous personality, namely the military officer Tjanuni. His Theban tomb (TT 74) is situated near the summit of the hill called Sheikh Abd el-Qurna. Its construction was begun under Amenhotep II, as some bricks and seals discovered here suggest, but the decoration of its walls dates, according to its style, from the reign of his son and successor Tuthmosis IV. As is usually the case with tombs from this period, it was never completed, only the entrance and the transversal hall having been painted.

Tjanuni was evidently of humble descent; his parents are nowhere mentioned. He may have owed his career in part to his wife Mutiri, a chantress of Thoth and, hence, probably from Hermopolis, who was a lady-in-waiting at the court. But Tjanuni himself was doubtless a competent administrator. Some information concerning his life is recorded on a stela in the tomb, which is, however, unfortunately rather lacunary.

He first followed Tuthmosis III on his campaigns into Syro-Palestine, from where, he states, "he brought back the princes of Djahi (Northern Palestine) as captives to Egypt, having conquered their towns and cut down their trees". Tjanuni continues: "It was I who recorded the victories which he (the king) made in all foreign counties – putting (it) in writing as it happened". That means that he was the author, or at least one of the authors, of the famous *Annals* of Tuthmosis III which are inscribed on the walls of the Karnak Temple.

Tjanuni carries on by stating that he "followed the Good God, the King of Upper and Lower Egypt, Aakheperure (Amenhotep II)", whose confidant he claims to have been. That may not be a pure *cliché*. He records various court titles among his epithets, and seems in these years to have married his wife who belonged to the court, and in whose tomb-shaft in TT 74 wine-jars were found inscribed with the name of Amenhotep II.

Under the succeeding Pharaoh, Tuthmosis IV, Tjanuni is said to have "noted down for him numerous soldiers". Several wall scenes depict the manner in which he supervised the inscription of the troops and the registration of the recruits, "causing that everyone in the entire army knew his duties". Another scene portrays an even more extensive inspection, of "soldiers, priests, servants of the king, all artisans of the land in its entirety", as well as of cattle, poultry, and small cattle. This is a task which slightly exceeds what one would expect from a military officer.

From various titles in the tomb the rise of Tjanuni through the hierarchical system is clear, although we do not hear at what precise moment he was every time promoted. He started out as a simple scribe, later becoming a royal scribe, that is, a low-level administrator. He climbed up to the position of "scribe of the recruits", one of the higher ranks in the army. It was in this capacity that he supervised the inspections that are depicted. Under Tuthmosis IV he ended his career as a general. Then the king gave him "a fine old age" and finally made for him a burial appropriate to a man of his status.

That Tjanuni was old when he died is certain. The bringing in of the captives from Djahi mentioned above probably occurred in year 29 of Tuthmosis III, while he lived well into the reign of Tuthmosis IV. If he was approximately twenty years old when he started out, he must have been at least seventy by the end of his career, possibly even over eighty. A front-line soldier he never had been – he nowhere records deeds of gallantry – but an efficient executive he remained until the end, when, according to his autobiography, "he noted down for the king his numerous soldiers". So we should rightly reckon Tjanuni, despite his military career, among the ranks of the aged administrators.

From the Nineteenth Dynasty we will first discuss the Viceroy of Kush (Nubia) called Setau. Although we do not know exactly how old he became, it is likely, in view of the large number of his monuments and their wide geographical distribution, that he lived into ripe old age. The earliest date that we have for him is year 38 of Ramesses II, which occurs on stelae from Wadi es-Sebua and Abu Simbel. The autobiographical text which he placed on another stela at Wadi es-Sebua is dated to year 44. Since on the earlier ones he is already recorded as Viceroy, one of the top positions in the state, he was certainly not young any more. So he must have been of approximately the same age as his king's reign.

One higher date that is attested for him occurs on a rock stela erected on the East Bank at Tonqala, North of Qasr Ibrim. Unfortunately, this date is badly damaged. Originally it was read as "year

63", but it could equally well be 39, 47, or 55. Whatever, there is no reason to suppose that this was the last year of Setau. He probably remained in office into his fifties, if not into his sixties, and may well have lived somewhat longer.

Setau is perhaps the most prolific private builder of the New Kingdom, particularly in his province of Nubia which he, in the words of one scholar, "cluttered with monuments". He constructed two temples, at Wadi es-Sebua and Gerf Hussein, and restored two others, at Amada and Ellesiya. All these sites are situated in Lower Nubia, the hub of Egyptian territory South of Aswan. Setau also founded two private chapels in this region, at Faras and Qasr Ibrim, which were devoted to the worship of his sovereign. To these can be added numerous stelae, statues, and rock inscriptions, totalling in all at least seventy-seven monuments. Clearly, this implies a timespan of at least fifteen to twenty years for the tenure of his office as Viceroy.

Yet, it is not only in Nubia that he left signs of his building activity. There are traces of a gateway that he erected at Memphis, and of a chapel, now lost, at Abydos. But the best known of his Egyptian monuments is another small chapel, measuring only 6 by 5 metres, which he constructed at el-Kab, out in the desert and well away from the town. It is known locally as el-Hammam, and was devoted to Thoth, Horus, and to Nekhbet, the vulture goddess of el-Kab. As was usual in that period, it also housed a cult statue of Ramesses II, Setau's master. There was a reason why he built a sanctuary at this site, which was situated outside his province – only just outside, in fact, for in those days the first two nomes of Upper Egypt down to Hierakonpolis, directly opposite el-Kab, also fell under the jurisdiction of the Viceroy. The explanation is that Setau's wife Nefertmut very probably originated from this town. At least she was a chantress of Nekhbet. Setau himself may have come from Thebes, where he was also buried. His tomb (TT 289) has not yet been published.

Setau tells us something about his career on one of the stelae he erected in the Temple of Wadi es-Sebua. He was educated at the court, and grew up in the palace. At a rather early age, perhaps in his twenties, he was already appointed chief of the Vizier's secretariat, a post in which he looked after the divine offerings and the granaries of Amun, which belonged under the authority of the Vizier. Then he was promoted to the function of Chief Steward of Amun which gave him independent power; in this position he also acted as Overseer of Amun's Treasury and Festival Leader of the god. It is from these years that a stela housed in the British Museum must date, for the title Viceroy is there still absent.

The next step was his appointment as Viceroy of Kush and Superintendent of the Gold Lands. In this function he was not only responsible for law and order in the large tracts of land in the South under Egypt's dominion, but also particularly for the sending of tribute to the capital, above all gold, but also valuable commodities from Central Africa. In this capacity Setau mentions a military action in which he captured a local chief together with his entire family and dispatched them to Egypt. One of his officers records, on another stela at Wadi es-Sebua, that people from the "lands of Tjemhu", West of the Nile, who seem to have been Libyans, were transported to work on the construction of the temple.

As stated above, that is the activity for which Setau is best known, in particular the building of the temple at Wadi es-Sebua and later that of Gerf Hussein. Both are of a hemispeos type, that is, partly cut into the rock. The former was dedicated to Re-Harakhte, and was embellished with a parallel row of lion-headed sphinxes along the middle passage, which occasioned its name (es-Sebua = "the lions"). The Gerf Hussein sanctuary was dedicated to Ptah and to Ramesses II himself. In contrast to the former it was poorly constructed and is now submerged under the waters of Lake Nasser, whereas the other temple has been moved and rebuilt on a spot two kilometres North of its original site.

Probably Setau resided as Viceroy in Buhen, as opposed to the traditional capital of the province at Aniba, for in Buhen a large number of his monuments have been discovered: a statue and fragments of several stelae. One better preserved stela, now in the British Museum, shows Setau kneeling before the goddess Renenutet, represented as a cobra. As the deity of fertility she symbolizes the produce of Nubia which Setau sent to Egypt. For, whatever his prolific building activities, this was the main duty of a Viceroy.

A contemporary of Setau was Prince Khaemwaset, the fourth son of Ramesses II. He must have been born in about the same year as the Viceroy, at the very beginning of his father's reign, as the third child of Isinofre, the king's second official consort (see p. 120). His eldest half-brother was the crown-prince Amenhikopshef, and Khaemwaset also had a full brother Ramesses and a sister Bentanat. The third son, born from the king's first wife Nefertari, had died young, but Amenhikopshef remained for a considerable time, until about regnal year 40, the heir apparent to the throne. When he died, he was succeeded by Prince Ramesses, until at least year 52, and then Khaemwaset became crown-prince. The situation lasted only a few years, since in year 55 or soon afterwards he too died, to be succeeded by the thirteenth son Merenptah, also a child of Isinofre, who would eventually become king. The other, older brothers were not considered eligible for this position because their mothers were of lower rank.

Khaemwaset may have been the crown-prince only a few years, but he was certainly for a long time one of the leading authorities in the state. His main function was that of High Priest of Ptah at Memphis. This was to him not a sinecure, as it could so easily have been for a son of the Pharaoh, but a position that he really held, from about his twenty-fifth year onwards. A military man like his elder brothers he seems never to have been, but as High Priest of Ptah he represented his father in the area, particularly when the ageing monarch became less active (see p. 120).

Khaemwaset was actually called on his monuments *sem* and "Great Chief of the Artisans", two titles of the High Priest. The latter indicates that he directed the so-called "gold-house", the workshop where the statues of valuable materials were made. In the representations he is usually shown with the youth-lock, the braided plait at one side of the head (fig. 54a), and clad in a leopard skin. This is the ancestral dress for a prince when he fulfils the duty of "opening the mouth" for his father's mummy. In that capacity he was called *sem*, and from the old ritual both the garment and the title of the Ptah-priest were derived.

Prince Khaemwaset is primarily known for three reasons. Firstly, he announced the first five *sed*-festivals of his father, for which he travelled through Upper Egypt (see p. 119). Very probably he also played a prominent rôle in the ceremonies themselves. Then, he rebuilt the Ptah Temple at Memphis, and erected a temple for the Apis bulls at the Serapeum at Saqqara. He also placed colossi of Ramesses II in front of the former. One of these is now standing in Ramses Square in Cairo, in front of the main railway station, while another is still lying, in a special building, close to its original site. On the former he is depicted in relief near the legs, his sister Bentanat being shown at the other side.

At the Serapeum he buried, as was the duty of the High Priest of Ptah, the Apis bulls. The first one, which died in year 30, was the last bull to receive its own isolated tomb. Then Khaemwaset constructed for the succeeding sacred animals what are known as the Lesser Vaults – the large galleries that can at present be visited date from the Twenty-Second Dynasty. In the smaller galleries remains which are supposed to belong to his own tomb have been discovered (fig. 54b), so that we may conclude that the prince was buried in the vicinity.

Elsewhere Khaemwaset also placed statues in the temples. A famous example is that in breccia from Abydos, which shows him standing with sacred staffs in both arms, that on the left side surmounted by the enigmatic symbol of Abydos. This sculpture is now one of the treasures of the British Museum.

Finally, Khaemwaset is also famous because he was a scholar, the earliest archaeologist whom we know of. He was interested in the

Khaemwaset: (above) upper part of a yellow limestone statuette ?of this prince (Unprovenanced, Nineteenth Dynasty); (right) black steatite headless shabti (?Tomb of Khaemwaset at Saqqara, Nineteenth Dynasty). (Fig. 54)

builders of the many pyramids and tombs at Giza and Saqqara, and left on them inscriptions stating that he had restored them. This will not mean more than that he made minor restorations, but the main purpose was to keep the ancient names alive.

A striking proof of this facet of his personality was discovered at Memphis. It is a fragmentary statue of Kawab, the eldest son of Pharaoh Khufu (see p. 16), which bears an inscription from the Nineteenth Dynasty. This relates how it was found by Khaemwaset in Kawab's tomb at Giza, evidently still intact, and brought to the Ptah Temple. Possibly it was not the only one.

From such scientific activities Khaemwaset received his later fame as a magician, in which capacity he is the leading character in the Demotic *Stories of Setne*. The events told here bear little relation to the historical High Priest, but that the latter was one of the great administrators of his time is certain.

Let us now descend from the lofty realms of a Prince and a Viceroy to look at an executive in the community of workmen at Deir el-Medina (see pp. 8-9 and *passim*). He was called Qenhikhopshef, and his title was "scribe (that is, administrator) of the necropolis". In that capacity he supervised the delivery of provisions to the men and their families as well as the work in the Royal Tomb itself.

Qenhikhopshef occurs for the first time in an ostracon from year 40 of Ramesses II, but he could have been appointed a decade earlier. His appalling handwriting is very conspicuous and as such can be easily recognized. Its characteristics can be seen in another ostracon dated to year 31, so that he may well have functioned from approximately year 30. He remained in office until year 6 of Seti II, sixty years later. If he was about twenty when he was nominated, he was therefore approximately eighty years old when he died.

He was the son of a workman, but in his youth he was adopted by a childless couple, the necropolis scribe Ramose and his wife (see p. 89). On the pass above the Valley of the Kings, along a path from Deir el-Medina to the Royal Tombs, a group of stone huts can still be seen in which the workmen passed the night. The most spacious of these belonged to Qenhikhopshef. On a stone seat discovered there a mention occurs of the scribe Ramose, followed by the words: "his son, who makes his name alive, the scribe Qenhikhopshef". Clearly, the latter honoured the name of his adoptive father in later years.

In other respects he seems not to have been such a decent person. In the papyrus in which the crimes of Paneb are enumerated (see pp. 89-90) there is a record that this chief workman bribed him, and in an ostracon formerly in the Gardiner collection and now in the Ashmolean Museum, we read that the workman Rahotep shaved Qenhikhophef's hair, "and gave him 15 cubits of cloth and 9 fathoms of yarn, after he had concealed his (Rahotep's) crimes". Bribery was certainly not considered a serious offence in those days, but our scribe seems rather to have overdone it.

Ramose, his adoptive parent, was obviously comfortably off; he built no less than three tombs at Deir el-Medina (TT 7, 212, and 250), and he erected several stelae and statues. This wealth Qenhikhopshef would have inherited, and he seems to have invested part of it in a library, some of the papyri of which were still in the possession of future generations of the family.

One of these papyri bears three different texts. When he acquired it, the document was covered on the recto by a "Dream-Book", a list of subjects that can appear in dreams, each accompanied by a statement concerning its quality (good or bad) and an interpretation. A few examples will suffice to make clear what is meant by this:

towing a boat:	good;	his landing happily at home.
threshing grain upon the threshing floor:	good;	the giving of life to him in his house.

or:

looking into a deep well:	bad;	his being put in prison.
removing the nails of his fingers:	bad;	removal of the work of his hands.

These examples are more or less rational, but others remain mysterious:

the gods making tears cease for him:	bad;	it means fighting.
eating hot meat:	bad;	it means his not being found innocent.

The second text, which Qenhikhopshef himself wrote on the blank verso of this papyrus, is a copy of a poem on the Battle of Qadesh, which he could find inscribed on the walls of several temples in the neighbourhood. He must have noted it down many years after the event, in the time of Merenptah. This text is proof of his great interest in history, which is also aptly demonstrated by an ostracon containing the names of twelve Pharaohs of the Eighteenth and Nineteenth Dynasties, with on the other side those of Montuhotep II Nebhepetre and Horemhab. The execrable handwriting is again unmistakably that of our scribe. Similar lists of royal names occur on his offering table in Marseilles, and on another papyrus which bears a ritual of Amenhotep I, who as patron of Deir el-Medina had a chapel in the vicinity.

The third text of the Dream-Book papyrus is a letter written by Qenhikhopshef to the Vizier of Merenptah, Panehsy, concerning the affairs of the workmen's community. Other such letters, of an earlier date, are known from ostraca. They are either drafts or copies, for the originals were of course sent away. They prove that the sender, although merely a local administrator, stayed in close contact with one of the heads of government. The reason is that the Vizier had responsibility for the supervision of Pharaoh's tomb and of its workmen; he was Qenhikhopshef's immediate boss.

From our scribe's hand is also a prophylactic charm on a sheet of papyrus, now in the British Museum. The spell is directed against a

Limestone head-rest decorated with fabulous creatures (Tomb of Qenhikhopshef at Deir el-Medina, Nineteenth Dynasty). (Fig. 55)

demon called Sehaqeq who appears to be threatening him. Qenhikhopshef identifies himself with an obscure deity in an attempt to ward off the evil power. He indicates that the incantation should be recited over a stem of flax, which would then be used as an arrow, the sheet of papyrus being folded and attached to it.

To the same magical sphere belongs an elaborate limestone headrest which once formed part of the funeral equipment of Qenhikhopshef's tomb (fig. 55). The burial place itself, certainly somewhere in the Valley of Deir el-Medina, has long been destroyed, but some elements from it survive. The headrest, which is less than ten centimetres in height, is on one side decorated with Bes figures. The other side, illustrated here, shows left a griffin with a lotus flower on its head, and right a lioness devouring a snake. Both creatures are armed with knives. They are reminiscent of the designs on ivory apotropaeic wands that play a rôle in pregnancy magic. An inscription on the headrest, now partly illegible, contains the words "good sleeping in the West, the Land of Righteousness" and the name of the owner, which shows that the object was not used in daily life.

Whether Qenhikhopshef married in his youth we do not know. He nowhere mentions the name of a wife or a child. In his old age, however, he found happiness with a very young bride, barely old enough to be his granddaughter. She was called Naunakhte (see p. 96). Soon she would become a widow, inheriting part of his property, including his beloved library. Clearly she was fond of the old man, for when she remarried she named her first son after him.

So we can see that Qenhikhopshef was a distinct personality with varying traits: prone to be seduced by bribery, believing in magical forces, but also devoted to the child-wife of his latter days. We can best picture him as an old man sitting on his seat cut out of the rock above the tomb of Merenptah, from where he could supervise the activities of his workmen. An inscription there perpetuates his name and titles. Sadly, however, the seat is in recent years no longer visible, being covered by an extensive mound of rubble. Nevertheless, the picture can live on in the imagination.

Finally, we present a long-lived celebrity who flourished at the end of Egypt's independent rule. This is Udjahorresnet ("Horus of Resnet is prosperous", Resnet being a chapel in the Temple of Neith at Sais), who became chief physician under the first Persian rulers of the so-called Twenty-Seventh Dynasty. Most of what we know about him derives from his green basalt, naophorous statue that originally stood in Sais and is now in the Vatican Museum (fig. 56). It is almost completely covered in texts, and dates from the very beginning of the reign of King Darius, *circa* 520 B.C.

Udjahorresnet began his career, according to his biographical account, under Pharaoh Amasis, the last great ruler of the Twenty-Sixth Dynasty. He then occupied the position of Commander of the Fleet. Hence, he would already have been middle-aged; what he did earlier he does not tell us. His father, Peftuaneith, was a priest of Neith at Sais, and in view of the later career of Udjahorresnet it is evident that he received a scholarly and priestly education. Yet, he may have been from a family with a military tradition, the combination not being exceptional in those days.

Udjahorresnet remained a fleet commander during the short reign of Psammetichus III. Then, in 525 B.C., the Persians conquered Egypt. As the biography laconically states: "The Great King of all foreign lands, Cambyses, came to Egypt". Not a word is uttered concerning any defence against the invaders, as one would expect from an admiral, nor about the misery that is wont to accompany such a conquest. In two separate, short inscriptions on the statue, however, in which the author sets forth how admirably he cared for the people in his city as well as for his own family, he speaks of the days "when the cataclysm befell his nome (of Sais), in the midst of the very great cataclysm which happened in the entire land". This certainly refers to the events which are suppressed in the main story.

That text deals predominantly with the period of Persian rule. First we are told that Cambyses appointed our former military officer to be his chief physician, and induced him to live at the court as a Companion and Director of the Palace. As the king's favourite he made himself useful by composing Cambyses' Egyptian royal titulary and names.

All this may surprise us. The Greek "Father of History" Herodotus, writing in *circa* 450 B.C., and following him other classical authors, tell us that Cambyses behaved in Egypt as a monster of depravity. This culminated in his slaughter of the sacred Apis bull. That story dates, however, from later years when, after a short period of freedom, the Egyptians were again shackled under an alien yoke. Also we must ask the question as to whether it was Cambyses' action against the revenues of the temples which had stirred up such bitter feelings in priestly circles. From Udjahorresnet's record we gain the impression of an attempt by Cambyses to reconcile the Egyptians to his régime, by assimilating his activities to the traditional model of Egyptian kingship. That appears evident from what follows. Hence, Udjahorresnet was not the collaborator he has sometimes been accused of being, an abject Quisling who betrayed his own people, but rather a wise statesman who fully supported his sovereign in his policy of reconciliation.

He told the king, he relates on his statue, about the greatness of Sais and the Temple of Neith and pleaded with him to remove the foreigners who had settled in the complex. Indeed, the alien ruler commanded that they be expelled and, after their houses had been demolished and their belongings carried off, the temple was cleansed. The divine offerings were restored, festivals and processions again installed, and the priesthood reorganized. All this took place under Udjahorresnet's supervision, as he records in another text on the statue. Then he entreated Cambyses to come himself to Sais, as a final act of reconciliation. This the Persian did, prostrating himself before Neith, and offering to her, as well as venerating the other deities in the temple, particularly the local form of Osiris.

The biography then jumps to the reign of the next Persian ruler Darius. It appears that Udjahorresnet had gone to Persia, presumably as a doctor. Whether he did this voluntarily or not is unclear. Darius now ordered him to return to Egypt, to restore the office of the House of Life at Sais. This is the scriptorium in which the sacred books were copied and studied, and where new ones were composed. Some of them deal not with religious matters but with what we would call science: astronomy, medicine, and so on. The study had its practical implications, for one of Darius' reasons for the restoration was that "he knew the usefulness of this craft for causing the sick to live and in order to cause to endure the names of all the gods, their temples, their offerings, and the conduct of their festivals for ever". Our physician was enabled to provide the renewed institution with students "who were the sons of well-born men,

Green basalt naophorous statue of Udjahorresnet. H. 69 cm. Head and hands modern (Sais, Twenty-Seventh Dynasty). (Fig. 56)

no low-born among them, and he placed scholars in charge of them to teach them".

So much for this statue. We possess some further evidence concerning Udjahorresnet, but it is all rather vague. In the early

Nineteenth Century A.D., one of Jean-François Champollion's travelling companions, Ippolito Rosellini, glimpsed a statue somewhere in Cairo. He copied parts of its inscriptions, only being interested in those in which a cartouche occurred. It seems to have been a sculpture much alike that in the Vatican, of a similar size and relating the same facts. At least, the self-same kings and identical phrases were recorded on it. Unfortunately, no trace of it has ever subsequently been discovered.

In 1956 there came to light at Memphis the torso of a statue bearing a most interesting text. It was made 177 years after the death of Udjahorresnet, when a statue of him had been found decaying. Therefore, this new one was fashioned. This teaches us that Udjahorresnet was a celebrated character long after his death.

In the late eighties, the Czech expedition excavating at Abusir located a tomb which turned out to belong to our physician. It was built at a lonely spot in the desert, at some distance South of the Abusir pyramids; later on it attracted other burials in the area. The discovery contained a mystery, for it appears that the inner sarcophagus, although it was sealed, had never been used for the mummy.

We must now leave the reader of this long chapter with the anticipation that further news concerning this sensational find may be expected. However, the damper is that, as with so much funerary archaeology, we are, until now, not much wiser about Udjahorresnet himself, who was doubtless one of the last great aged administrators of Egyptian history.

Postscript
A Centenarian Egyptologist

In A.D. 1963 an Egyptologist was to beat the record of Ramesses II and equal the alleged age of Pepi II by reaching a century. Dr. (Miss) Margaret Murray (1863-1963) is the only Egyptologist to have done so, although it is a discipline which clearly attracts longevity as women such as Gertrude Caton-Thompson and Elizabeth Riefstahl have lived into their late nineties. In order to add one man, mention can be made of the American archaeologist Dows Dunham who died at the age of ninety-three.

In 1959 Margaret Murray had the unnerving experience of reading that she was dead! She at once wrote a witty and well-formulated rejoinder to the national newspaper in question, and the faded yellow clipping still survives in her personal file in the archives of the Petrie Museum. Printed under the heading "Very Much Alive", it deserves to be quoted in full:

> Sir—Miss Stevie Smith in her review headed 'In Defence of Witches' (February 15), refers to 'the late Dr. Margaret Murray'. I was not aware till then that I was dead. Perhaps she or some of your readers can inform me when and where I died, for the event appears to have slipped from my memory.

The comment of the abashed editor appears below: "Miss Stevie Smith asks us to add her apologies to our own".

Here is not the place to discuss Margaret Murray's long career, information on which can be found in the literature cited in the bibliography at the end of this book. Instead our concentration will be on her activities as a nonagenarian. However, this may be a suitable point to quote verbatim the resolution passed by the Professorial Board at University College London (UCL) on the 11th June 1963, to record its thanks and appreciation to Margaret Murray, as this gives an excellent summary of her achievements:

> That on the occasion of Dr. Margaret Murray's 100th birthday, they wish to place on record their deep appreciation of the high

*Margaret Murray, aged
sixty-eight, wearing her
doctoral robes of 1931.
(Fig. 57)*

honour which, through her renowned scholarship, she has brought
to University College London, where she taught for so many years.
Trained in her early Egyptological study by Sir Flinders Petrie, Dr.
Murray became his 'right hand', and in relieving him of a great
part of his teaching work in the College, she made possible the vast
output of his work in the field; Sir Flinders Petrie was always first in
acknowledging his debt to her. And there were others: scholars of
international repute such as Wainwright, Brunton, Engelbach,
Starkey, Lankester Harding and Faulkner, who owed their early
training at the College to Dr. Murray.

In her own research, she was just as successful as in her teaching.
Books and articles, both scientific and popular, have come from her
pen, not only on Egyptology, but in many other fields, such as her
latest book, *The Genesis of Religion*, published in this year, the hundredth of her long life. In addition to this, Dr. Murray's excavations
at the Osireion at Abydos, and her epigraphic work in the necropolis at Sakkara are recognized as monumental contributions to
Egyptological research.

The Professorial Board desires to express to Dr. Murray its
thanks for all she has done for the College, not only during the long

period of her service on its academic staff but also for her valuable association with its Department of Egyptology, in which her interest still continues long after her official retirement.

An illuminator was commissioned to prepare this resolution for presentation to Dr. Murray at her hundredth birthday celebration luncheon held at UCL on the 15th July 1963 (see fig. 59). Elegantly inscribed on vellum, in black, red, blue, and burnished gold, the citation now resides in the College Library.

As indicated in the resolution, Margaret Murray was still busily writing in her hundredth year. In fact, despite being badly crippled by arthritis, two books were published in 1963, the second of which was her autobiography *My First Hundred Years* (first announced under the original title *A Century in View*). One wonders if there have been any other centenarians with such a prolific output?

Indeed, following her official retirement from UCL in 1935 at the age of seventy-two, she had refused to "go to that uncomfortable and flat resting place" – the shelf – and had set out to actively pursue her literary career. She then published six more books, including *The Splendour of Egypt*, a permanent bestseller which appeared on her eighty-sixth birthday – "A fact of which I think I may be proud".

Her enormous output in the fields of both Egyptology and folklore amounted to getting on for a hundred and fifty books and articles. She herself kept no record of her published works for, when one was finished, she at once proceeded with the next. Not surprisingly, this caused considerable difficulties to her 1961 bibliographer, who could by no means be certain that he had managed to track down all her articles, and wisely decided to omit her reviews as being too difficult to trace.

When she was ninety-seven Margaret Murray had written an article for the prestigious archaeological periodical *Antiquity* entitled "First Steps in Archaeology". In his editorial of this issue Dr. Glyn Daniel stated that they had "immediately commissioned her to write another article for the June 1963 number of *Antiquity*". "Centenary" was duly delivered without any further reminder or urging, to the delight of the editor who could only lament: "If only our younger contributors would be so faithful and forthcoming!"

Margaret Murray was always poor. Until 1922 her salary was only £200 per annum, and despite bearing the brunt of the teaching load in Petrie's absence, she had been forced to undertake much outside lecturing in order to literally double her income. In 1931 her devoted students had clubbed together to pay for her gown when she was awarded her honorary doctorate (fig. 57). Naturally, she then retired on

Margaret Murray, aged ninety-seven, on the steps of the portico at University College London (1960). (Fig. 58)

an inadequate pension which compelled her to continue to conduct numerous evening classes well into her eighties. Many of her pupils were themselves elderly ladies; she was once asked why she spent so much time with such students. She had so much to do in terms of research and publishing, whereas they, by contrast, were never going to be Egyptologists and were not even particularly interested. The witty retort was: "Ah, my dear, the important thing is: when I've got them here, they can't get into mischief".

146

Her encouragement of all pupils, even the miscellaneous crowd of women of a certain age, was noteworthy, as was her endless patience. Countless generations of students remember the very welcoming and friendly atmosphere of one or other of her London 'bed-sits', where they would gather cosily around the fire and listen to her entertaining stories of witchcraft or excavations. For over sixty years she was, as she termed it, a "paying-guest" in one of such establishments in the environs of UCL. In 1960, aged ninety-seven she had to vacate the house in 16 Endsleigh Street where she had resided since the forties and find somewhere else to live for six months. She fully admitted that this was not easy as people did not want the responsibility of a person of her age.

Margaret Murray loved children. In her late eighties she became a great favourite with the son of one of her *protégés*, who regarded her as an extra grandmother. She would give him little trinkets – bits of lapis lazuli, a Roman lamp, some beads from Egypt – and each time tell him a little about them. He in turn would put them religiously in his treasure box.

She is still an unforgettable figure to those who were at the College in the fifties and early sixties (fig. 58). Many people remember to this day the picture of the tiny four foot ten *(circa* 1.47 metres) frame of this former suffragette alongside the towering six foot two (almost 1.90 metres) figure of Professor W.B. Emery, who was at that time the incumbent of the Edwards Chair of Egyptology. The stories surrounding her at this time are legendary; two will have to suffice here.

Professor Emery visited her in University College Hospital after an emergency appendicitis operation performed when she was in her nineties. He found her ensconced in her own private room, already sitting up in bed and typing furiously. That morning, she informed him, the French police had visited her, seeking her advice on a case of witchcraft in their country. Indeed, she had become a celebrated, albeit highly controversial authority on the subject, her *The Witch-Cult in Western Europe* (1921) being described as "revolutionary" and "epoch-making".

The second anecdote concerns another visit to her by Emery, accompanied by his secretary, which took place in May 1962 when she was nearly ninety-nine. Just as they were leaving she remarked: "You know I've got an incurable disease?". Thinking that something very serious had developed, they were understandably relieved when she continued: "Yes, old age".

Whatever, Margaret Murray's mind continued to remain as clear and active as ever throughout her nineties. At all times she took a lively interest in College affairs in general and of the Egyptology Department in particular. Until the age of ninety-four when the many stairs began to defeat her, she appeared regularly in the Department, occasionally invading a language class, and invariably wanting to see a particular object in the museum.

The Petrie Museum archives contain a series of letters from the 1960s exchanged between Margaret Murray and Professor Emery, or, in his absence on excavation, his secretary Miss Cynthia Cox. They show her delight in her particular fields of research to be undimmed, and as such it is a joy which is infectious as one shares her excited zest for discovery. She is mainly writing about her "bit of research on the Hierakonpolis finds, with what are, to me, surprising results". (She regarded this excavation as one of the three to have revolutionized Egyptology at the turn of the century). In one letter she tells Emery: "I have now identified the serpopard, and am on the trail of the seraph (the hawk-headed winged leopard)".

At the end of 1961 she was admitted to the Queen Victoria Hospital at Welwyn in Hertfordshire, following an acute attack of arthritis. She was to stay here for the remainder of her life. In 1962 she writes to Emery: "I do appreciate the feeling that I can keep in touch with Egyptologists and know the advances that are being made, and I hope that before long I also may make a small contribution, and be again one of the splendid band of researchers. I wish for all of you good luck in your research and the fun of 'finding out'".

Margaret Murray reading her citation at her hundredth birthday celebration at University College London (July 1963). (Fig. 59)

148

Her final two letters, dating from February and September 1963, show her dream to have come true. Her characteristic large, round hand has now sadly deteriorated to a shaky scrawl, but she is still desperate for information. The last letter is indeed remarkable and deserves to be quoted in full:

Dear Professor Emery,
I am writing to ask some help on my Hierakonpolis work. It is about the temple. Is the revetment of any real importance for the early buildings, and are there any buildings, except the Painted Tomb, of the date of Scorpion? What date is the revetment that bulks so largely in Green's plans and letterpress?

Also, would you agree that Aha as Menes is a combination of Scorpion and Narmer? ... (The next sentence is illegible) ... Also there are I think three *serekhs,* each of which has a large hieroglyph associated with it. All these might well be titles of the <u>functions</u> of different important offices held by one man. I claim these three *serekhs* all belong to one man, Mena-Nar, the Founder of the 'United Kingdom'.

There are other bits of evidence to support this theory which you have already suggested for Mena-Aha, but not I think with sufficiently strong evidence. I therefore want to give the credit of the suggestion to the right quarter.

Emery's long handwritten draft reply is appended. He tells her of an Archaic inscription of a scorpion noted in Nubia during his last campaign. "During the coming season I intend to make tracings and rubbings and I think we will find something very interesting indeed. I will keep you informed. Definite evidence of Scorpion in Nubia would indeed be a sensation". Alas, Margaret Murray would never know the outcome, as she died two months after this letter was written.

One further missive is found among the series. Dated to January 1962 it is a reply to Cynthia Cox who had forwarded a letter from someone who "evidently wants to become an active member of a local coven". Margaret Murray replies in characteristic fashion. "What asses there are in the world! I have replied to that idiot, whose letter you forwarded, with a snorter!"

"We shall certainly run the flag to the top of the mast to mark what must be a unique occasion in the annals of the College". This took place on Monday 15th July 1963, two days after Margaret Murray's birthday, when the centenarian was brought by her doctor to UCL for the celebration buffet luncheon. Margaret Murray's preparations had involved a consultation with the Queen's hat designer, who had visited her at the Hospital with a selection from his range. She arrived for her party wearing a very fetching toque (fig. 59). Surrounded by thirty of her friends and pupils, she managed, despite her deafness and the confines of a wheelchair, to talk to many people, fully remembering everyone. At the appropriate moment the College Chef ceremoniously carried in the cake which had been designed by Margaret Drower, who was later to become Petrie's definitive biographer. Decorated in marzipan were her initials "M.A.M." together with the appropriate hieroglyphs for "life, prosperity, and health".

After receiving her citation, the centenarian made a short speech of acknowledgement and departed from UCL for the last time. Despite her doctor Charles Dansie writing on the 19th July that "Dr. Murray has had a few quiet days and is now getting down to the second century in her usual fashion", this was not to be. Exactly four months after her birthday, on the 13th November 1963, this indefatigable character, who still took the greatest interest in everything, finally died.

It will come as no surprise that Margaret Murray had left strict instructions as to the nature of her funeral. Throughout her life she had held an abiding horror of high churches. Her funeral therefore was to be "of the plainest kind, without any Romish or High Church extravagances. No wreaths or flowers to be given in remembrance of me". At the end of the service she requested "some cheerful hymn and a gay and lively recessional voluntary".

In her hundredth year Margaret Murray followed the discoveries of the space age with as much zest as she had given to the invention of the bicycle. As she herself said: "I have lived through one of the most momentous periods of that miracle of world-history, the advance of Man". Indeed, she had witnessed the growth of archaeology practically from its beginnings. When she was born in 1863 the acceptance of the antiquity of man and the publication of Darwin's *The Origin of Species* was only four years old.

The last tribute will be left to her physician quoted above who shortly before her death wrote: "To have known Dr. Murray is in itself the best reward for looking after her – she has added greatly to the fullness of our lives in the past two years".

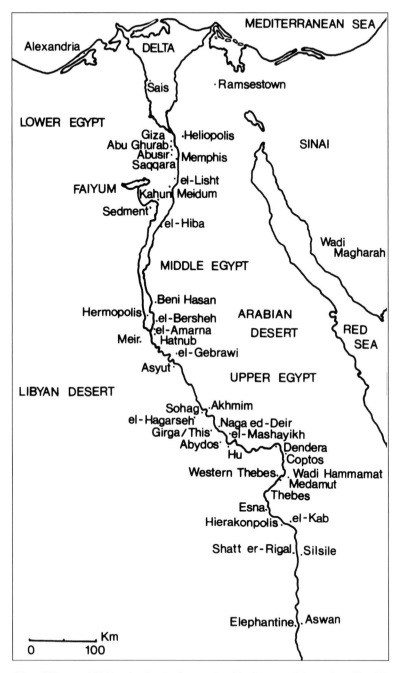

Map of Egypt and Nubia, showing the sites mentioned in the text and the captions (Fig. 60)

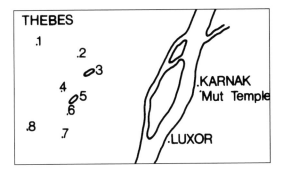

Key to map of Thebes:
    1. Valley of the Kings; 2. Deir el-Bahri;
    3. Sheikh Abd el-Qurna; 4. Deir el-Medina;
    5. Qurnet Murai; 6. Medinet Habu;
    7. Malkata; 8. Valley of the Queens.

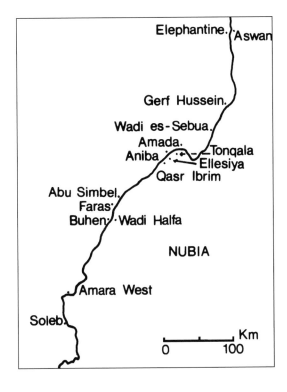

Detailed maps of Thebes and Nubia, showing the sites mentioned in the text and the captions (Fig. 61)

153

List of Museums

(mostly mentioned in the text under toponyms)

Aswan	:	Aswan Museum (Elephantine Island).
Baltimore	:	The Walters Art Gallery.
Berlin	:	Staatliche Museen zu Berlin. Ägyptisches Museum und Papyrussammlung (Bode-Museum).
Boston	:	Museum of Fine Arts.
Cairo	:	Egyptian Museum/Musée Egyptien.
Cambridge	:	Fitzwilliam Museum.
Chicago	:	Field Museum of Natural History.
	:	The Oriental Institute Museum, University of Chicago.
Geneva	:	Musée d'Art et d'Histoire.
Glasgow	:	Hunterian Museum, University of Glasgow.
Hildesheim	:	Roemer-Pelizaeus Museum.
Kansas City	:	The Nelson-Atkins Museum of Art.
Leiden	:	Rijksmuseum van Oudheden.
Liverpool	:	School of Archaeology and Oriental Studies, University of Liverpool.
London	:	The British Museum.
	:	The Petrie Museum of Egyptian Archaeology, University College London.
Luxor	:	The Luxor Museum of Egyptian Art.
Marseilles	:	Musée d'Archéologie Méditerranéenne.
Moscow	:	The Pushkin Museum of Fine Arts.
Munich	:	Staatliche Sammlung Ägyptischer Kunst.
New York	:	The Brooklyn Museum.
	:	The Metropolitan Museum of Art.
Oxford	:	Ashmolean Museum.
Paris	:	Musée du Louvre.
Philadelphia	:	Pennsylvania University Museum.
Rome	:	Museo Gregoriano Egizio (Vatican).
Turin	:	Museo Egizio.

Select Bibliography

Lexikon der Ägyptologie. Begründet von Wolfgang Helck und Eberhard Otto, 6 vols., Wiesbaden, 1972-1986.

Lichtheim, Miriam, *Ancient Egyptian Literature*, 3 vols., Berkeley, 1973-1980.

II– Gerontology

Bond, John and Coleman, Peter (ed.), *Ageing in Society.* An Introduction to Social Gerontology, London, 1990.

Tinker, Anthea, *Elderly People in Modern Society*, 3rd ed., London, 1992.

Amos, P.T. and Harrel, S. (ed.), *Others Ways of Growing Old*, Stanford, California, 1981.

Kertzer, D.I. and Keith, J. (ed.), *Age and Anthropological Theory*, London, 1984.

III – Special Subjects
(in the order of the chapters)

Chapter I

Ryder, Arthur W., *The Panchatantra*. Translation from the Sanskrit, Chicago and London, 1972.

Omlin, Jos. A., *Der Papyrus 55001 und seine satirisch-erotische Zeichnungen und Inschriften*, Turin, 1973.

Chapter II

Ward, William A., Neferhotep and his Friends, *Journal of Egyptian Archaeology* 63 (1977), 63-66.

Riefstahl, E., An Egyptian Portrait of an Old Man, *Journal of Near Eastern Studies* 10 (1951), 65-73.

CHAPTER III

Cockburn, A. and E. (ed.), *Mummies, Diseases and Ancient Cultures*, Cambridge, 1980.

Podzorski, Patricia V., *Their Bones Shall Not Perish*. An examination of Predynastic Human Skeletal Remains from Naga-ed-Dêr in Egypt, New Malden, 1990.

CHAPTER IV

James, T.G.H., *The Hekanakhte Papers and Other Early Middle Kingdom Documents*, New York, 1962.

Whale, Sheila, *The Family in the Eighteenth Dynasty of Egypt*, Sydney, 1989.

Demarée, R.J., *The 3h ikr n R'-Stelae*. On Ancestor Worship in Ancient Egypt, Leiden, 1983.

CHAPTER V

Keith-Bennett, Jean L., Anthropoic Busts II. Not from Deir el Medineh Alone. *Bulletin of the Egyptological Seminar* 3 (1981), 43-71.

Gardiner, Alan H. and Sethe, Kurt, *Egyptian Letters to the Dead*. Mainly from the Old and Middle Kingdom, London, 1928.

Schneider, Hans D., *Een brief voor Anchiry*. Scenes uit een Egyptisch huwelijk, Zutphen, n.d.

CHAPTER VI

Janssen, J.M.A., On the Ideal Lifetime of the Egyptians, *Oudheidkundige Mededelingen uit het Rijksmuseum van Oudheden te Leiden* 31 (1950), 33-43.

CHAPTER VII

Hassan, Ali, *Stöcke und Stäbe im Pharaonischen Ägypten bis zum Ende des Neuen Reiches*, Munich/Berlin, 1976.

Blumenthal, Elke, Ptahhotep und der 'Stab des Alters', in: *Form und Mass*. Festschrift für Gerhard Fecht. Herausgegeben von Jürgen Osing und Günter Dreyer, Wiesbaden 1987, 84-97.

CHAPTER VIII

Blumenthal, Elke, Die 'Gottesväter' des Alten und Mittleren Reiches, *Zeitschrift für ägyptische Sprache und Altertumskunde* 114 (1987), 10-35.

Brunner, Hellmut, Der 'Gottesvater' als Erzieher des Kronprinzen, *Zeitschrift für ägyptische Sprache und Altertumskunde* 86 (1961), 90-100.

Kees, Hermann, 'Gottesväter' als Priesterklasse, *Zeitschrift für ägyptische Sprache und Altertumskunde* 86 (1961), 115-125.

Habachi, Labib, God's Fathers and the Role They Played in the History of the First Intermediate Period, *Annales du Service des Antiquitiés de l'Égypte* 55 (1958), 167-190.

CHAPTER IX

Gardiner, Alan H., Adoption Extraordinary, *Journal of Egyptian Archaeology* 26 (1940), 23-29.

Simpson, William Kelly, Polygamy in Egypt in the Middle Kingdom, *Journal of Egyptian Archaeology* 60 (1974), 100-105.

Kanawati, Naguib, Polygamy in the Old Kingdom? *Studien zur altägyptischen Kultur* 4 (1976), 149-160.

CHAPTER XI

Hornung, Erik und Staehelin, Elisabeth *et al.*, *Studien zum Sedfest* (= Aegyptiaca helveltica I), Geneva, 1974.

Kaiser, Werner, Die kleine Hebseddarstellung im Sonnentempel des Neuserre, *Beiträge zur ägyptischen Bauforschung und Altertumskunde* 12 (= Festschrift Herbert Ricke), Wiesbaden, 1971.

Uphill, E.P., The Egyptian Sed-Festival Rites, *Journal of Near Eastern Studies* 24 (1965), 365-383.

Gohary, Jocelyn, *Akhenaten's Sed-Festival at Karnak*, London 1992.

Blackman, A.M., The Stela of Nebipusenwosret: British Museum No. 101, *Journal of Egyptian Archaeology* 21 (1935), 1-9.

Simpson, William K., The Sed Festival in Regnal Year 30 of Amenemhet III and the Periodicity of the Festival in Dynasty XII, *Journal of the American Research Center in Egypt* 2 (1963), 59-63.

Spalinger, Anthony, Dated Texts of the Old Kingdom, *Studien zur altägyptischen Kultur* 21 (1994), 275-319.

CHAPTER XII

Simpson, William Kelly, *The Terrace of the Great God at Abydos: The Offering Chapels of Dynasties 12 and 13*, New Haven and Philadelphia, 1974.

Brack, Annelies und Artur, *Das Grab des Tjanuni. Theban Nr. 74*, Mainz am Rhein, 1977.

Habachi, Labib, Setau the Famous Viceroy of Ramses II and his Career, in: *Sixteen Studies on Lower Nubia*, Cairo, 1981, 121-138.

Gomaà, Farouk, *Chaemwese. Sohn Ramses' II. und Hoherpriester von Memphis*, Wiesbaden, 1973.

Posener, G., *La première domination perse en Égypte*, Cairo, 1936.

Lloyd, Alan B., The Inscription of Udjahorresnet. A Collaborator's Testament, *Journal of Egyptian Archaeology* 68 (1982), 166-180.

POSTSCRIPT

Murray, Margaret, *My First Hundred Years*, London, 1963.

Janssen, Rosalind M., *The First Hundred Years*. Egyptology at University College London 1892-1992, London, 1992.

List of Tombs at Thebes
(Page numbers in italic refer to illustrations)

TT (= Theban Tomb, private)

3	Pashedu	i, 23, *24*
7	Ramose	136
11	Dhuti	22
34	Montuemhat	23
39	Puyemre	20, *21*
40	Amenhotep (Huy)	25, *71*, 71
50	Neferhotep	60, *61*
52	Nakht	21
61	Useramun	45
64	Heqaerneheh	83
74	Tjanuni	130, 131
78	Haremhab	*54*, 54
79	Menkheperresonb	45
81	Ineni	64
87	Nakhtmin	45
90	Nebamun	102, *104*
96	Sennefer	9, *10*
97	Amenemhat	76
100	Rekhmire	45, 92
107	Nefersekheru	119
131	Useramun	45, 75
155	Antef	21
192	Kheruef	119
212	Ramose	136
216	Neferhotep	*89*
217	Ipuy	24
226	Heqareshu	*82*, 82
250	Ramose	136
289	Setau	132
290	Irinefer	25
335	Nakhtamun	52

Index

Page numbers in italic refer to illustrations